A
POCKET GUIDE
TO SPELLING

Michael Temple

John Murray

Also by Michael Temple

A Pocket Guide to Written English

© Michael Temple 1985

First published 1985
by John Murray (Publishers) Ltd
50 Albemarle Street, London W1X 4BD

Reprinted 1986

Typeset by Fakenham Photosetting Ltd,
Fakenham, Norfolk
Printed and bound in Great Britain
by Richard Clay (The Chaucer Press) Ltd

British Library Cataloguing in Publication Data

Temple, Michael
    A Pocket Guide to Spelling.
    1. Spellers
    I. Title
    428.1   PE1145.2

ISBN 0–7195–4187–5 PBK net

CONTENTS

Acknowledgements

I am grateful to my wife for her valuable assistance and to my pupils, past and present, without whose errors I could not have written this booklet.

1

General advice

You can't spell?

Or you have particular problems?

What can you do to help yourself?

There is no single answer but here to start with is a basic strategy, a simple procedure likely to help *any* bad speller.

The check-list (see chapter 2)

Well over half the spelling errors made involve a mere 200 or so common words. These, starred in the check-list, should be learnt gradually – five or ten at a time – along with the words that you personally keep misspelling but need to use. Always check with the list or with a dictionary if you are at all unsure how to spell a word. Remember that spelling mistakes can start to 'look right' after a while.

Take special care when first spelling a word: otherwise you may continually have problems with it.

A simple learning method

- Study the word carefully and pronounce it slowly, preferably out loud. If necessary, break it up into syllables and concentrate on the part(s) of the word causing difficulty.
- Shut your eyes and try to picture the word.
- Check the spelling letter by letter.
- Write the word down from memory.
- Check it carefully, again letter by letter.

For persistent errors underline that part of the word which gives you

1

trouble and keep your own alphabetically arranged short-list of correct spellings of key words. (Sometimes it is worth using or inventing a memory aid, e.g. Stationery comes from the stationer's and has an 'e' as in envelopes.)

And what next?

The approach of this book is first to enable you to *diagnose* where your particular problems lie (see chapter 3) and to put these right by directing you to specific *rules*, explanations and remedial exercises. These rules, given in chapters 4, 5 and 7 to 11, can be tackled little by little or worked through in sequence until your errors are eliminated. (The book has been arranged in such a way that rules may be checked quickly or studied in depth.)

Secondly, this book tries to help you *understand* why words are spelt as they are. History is largely to blame and therefore knowing a little about the *history of spelling* (see chapter 6) and about the *formation and derivation* of words (see chapter 8) serves to explain the apparent chaos.

Wide, attentive *reading* will make you familiar with the look of words, and reading aloud – or recording yourself on a tape-recorder for a later dictation – can also be helpful. *Graded dictation exercises*, designed to test the main spelling problems, are provided in chapter 13. (You will need to record them first or ask someone to dictate them to you.)

Inevitably in the following text I have had to use some technical terms such as vowel and consonant. Explanations of all of these will be found in chapter 12.

2
Spelling check-list

The check-list includes words which are often confused such as affect and effect. The most commonly misspelt words have been starred. Where it seems helpful, words have been arranged in 'families'. Plurals are given on the same line. The '-ise' ending has been used throughout, though '-ize' may often be an alternative.

(Key: n. = noun; adj. = adjective; vb = verb)

abbreviate
abhorrent
abominable
abscess
absence
abyss
  abysmal
accelerate
  accelerator
*accept (receive;
  see except)
*accidentally
acclaim
  acclamation
accommodate
* accommodation
accompany
  accompaniment
accomplice
accomplish
accurately
aching
*achieve
  achievement

achieving
acknowledg(e)ment
acquaint
  acquaintance
acquiesce
acquire
  acquisition
acquit
  acquitted
acreage
*across
adaptation
*address
*adequate
adjacent
adjourn
admitted
  admittance
  admission
  admissible
advantageous
*advertisement
advice (n.)
advise (vb)

aerial
aerodrome
aeroplane
*affect (vb
  influence; see
  effect)
aggravate
*aggression
  aggressor
agreeing
* agreeable
aisle (in a church)
alcohol
allege
  allegiance
alleviate
alley(s) (lanes; see
  ally)
allotted
  allotment
allowed
  (permitted; see
  aloud)
all right (2 words;

alright is slang)

allusion
 (reference; see
 illusion)

ally, allies
 (friends; see
 alley(s))

*a lot of (3 words)

aloud (out loud;
 see allowed)

already (by now)

all ready (all are
 ready)

altar (in a church)

alter (change)

altogether
 (completely)

all together (all in
 one place)

although

amateur

*among

amount

analysis, analyses
 analyse (vb)

ancestor
 ancestry

angel (in heaven)

angle (corner)

annihilate

announce

annual
 annually

anonymous

antidote

apartment

appal

* appalling

apparatus

*apparent

*appealing

*appear

* appearance

approach

appropriate

approximately

*arctic

*arguing

*argument

arithmetic

arrangement

arrears

arrest

arrival

arrogant

article

ascent (upward
 climb; see
 assent)

ascertain

assassinate

assault

assent
 (agreement; see
 ascent)

associate

as well (2 words)

athletics
 athletically

*atmosphere

attached

attempt

attitude

attract

aural (heard; see
 oral)

author

automatically

autumn
 autumnal

awesome

*awful
 awfully

awkward

*bachelor

bail (in law and
 cricket; see
 bale)

balance

bale (bundle;
 jump out; see
 bail)

balloon

balloted

banisters

bankruptcy

bare
 (uncover(ed); see
 bear)

barrenness

base (basis; see
 bass)

basically

bass (in music;
 fish; see base)

bath (n.)

bathe (vb)

baton

battalion

bazaar

beach (shore; see
 beech)

bear (carry,
 endure; an
 animal; see
 bare)

*beautiful

* beautifully

beech (tree; see
 beach)

beggar

*beginning
 beginner

behaviour

beige

*belief

*believe

bench, benches

4

benefactor
*benefited
bereaved
besiege
bicycle
biscuit
blatant
board (plank; take meals; *see* bored)
boarder (lodger; *see* border)
boisterous
bored (weary with; made a hole; *see* board)
border (edge; *see* boarder)
born (at birth)
borne (carried, endured)
boycott
brake(s) (on a car; stop)
break (shatter; interval)
breath (n. air in lungs)
breathe (vb to draw air)
brief
Britain (the country)
Briton (person)
broach (to open; *see* brooch)
broken
brooch (ornament; *see* broach)
budgeted
building
burglar
buses

busily
* business (job, firm)
busyness (being busy)
buoy (in the sea)
by (near, at, with)
bye (in games)

calculator
calendar
calf, calves
calibre
camouflage
campaign
cancel
cancelled
cancellation
cannibal
cannon (gun)
canoeing
canon (of the church)
canvas (coarse cloth)
*canvass (seek votes, etc.)
capital (chief city; of the head)
Capitol (Roman and US building)
careers
*careful
* carefully
careless
cargo, cargoes
*Caribbean
caricature
carpentry
catalogue
catapult
catarrh
catastrophe(s)

category
caterpillar
ceiling
cellar
cemetery
centre
*century, centuries
cereal (e.g. wheat; *see* serial)
changeable
chaos
*character
characteristically
chauvinist
check (stop; test; squares)
cheque (bank draft, bill)
chief, chiefs
chimneys
chocolates
choose (present tense)
chose (past tense)
Christian
Christmas
chute (falling channel)
cigarette
circuit
citizens
climbed
clothes (garments)
cloths (pieces of cloth)
coarse (rough, harsh; *see* course)
cocoa
coconut
collaborate
collapse
collapsible
colleague

5

college
collision
colloquial
colonel (in the
  army)
colossal
colour
  colourful
  colourfully
column
coming
comedy
  comedian
  comedienne
  (female)
commemorate
commend
commerce
commission
commit
* committed
* committee
* commitment
commotion
*comparatively
*comparison
compel
  compelling
competent
competition
  competitor
complement (that
  which makes up;
  see compliment)
*completely
compliment
  (praise: see
  complement)
  complimentary
  (praising)
comprehensible
compulsory
concede

conceit
*conceive
*concentrate
condemn
conductor
conferred
  conference
conjure
  conjurer (or -or)
connoisseur
conqueror
conscience
* conscientious
* conscious
consensus
consistent
*conspiracy
  conspirator
constituency
*contemporary
controlled
controversial
convertible
coolly
correspondence
corroborate
corrupt
council (an
  assembly)
counsel (advice,
  advise)
councillor (of a
  district assembly)
counsellor
  (adviser)
counterfeit
courageous
course ('of
  course'; track;
  meal; series; see
  coarse)
courtesy
  courteous

crescendo(s)
*criticism
  critically
  cruelly
  curious
  curiosity
currant (berry)
current (flow
  of —; now)
currency
cylinder
cynic
  cynically
  cynicism
cypress (tree)
Cyprus (island)
Czechoslovakia

daily
dairy, dairies (for
  milk)
damage
  damaging
debt
  debtor
decease (death;
  see disease)
deceive
* deceit
*decided
* decision
*defence
  defensive
defer (postpone;
  see differ)
  deferring
*definite
* definitely
degradation
delicacy
  delicately
delightful
  delightfully

6

democracy
democratically
dependant (n. one
who depends on
another)
*dependent (adj.
depending on)
derelict
*descend
descendant
*describe
* description
descriptively
desert (barren
place; abandon;
merit; see
dessert)
desiccated
despair
* desperately
despise
despicable
dessert (sweet
course; see
desert)
*detached
deteriorate
deterred
deterrent
devastate
develop
* developed
* development
device (n. a
scheme)
devise (vb to work
out a plan)
diamond
diarrhoea
diary, diaries
(book)
died (stopped
living)

diesel
differ (be unlike;
see defer)
differed
different
difference
diffuse (spread
loosely)
digital
dilapidated
dilemma
dilettante
dimensions
dining (eating)
diner (one who
eats; see dinner)
dinghy, dinghies
(boat)
dingy (dirty-
coloured)
dinner (meal)
disabled
disability
disagreeing
disagreement
*disappear
disappearance
*disappoint
disappointment
disapprove
disarrange
*disastrous
disciple
discipline
disciplinary
discotheque
disease (illness;
see decease)
disguise
dishevelled
*disillusioned
disintegrate
disobeyed

disobedience
dispatch
*dissatisfied
disservice
dissimilar
dissolve
dissuade
doctor
doesn't (does not)
dose (e.g. of
medicine; see
doze)
doubt
doubtful
doubtfully
doze (sleep; see
dose)
draft (plan, bill;
see draught)
drastically
draught (of air,
beer, ship; see
draft)
drawers (chest
of —)
draws (he draws;
tied games;
attractions)
*drunkenness
dual (of two,
double)
duel (fight
between two)
*duly
dungeon
dutiful
dyed (coloured)
dyeing
dying (almost
dead)

earnest
easily

7

eccentric
echo, echoes
echoing
*ecstasy
eerie
eerily
*effect (result, to bring about; *see* affect)
effervescence
efficiency
eight
eighth
eighteen
eighty
either
*elegant
elegance
elicit (draw out; *see* illicit)
eligible (fit to be chosen; *see* illegible)
eligibility
eloquence
*embarrass
* embarrassment
embellish
emergency
emigrant (leaves the country; *see* immigrant)
eminent (prominent; *see* imminent)
emotion
*emperor
empress
emptiness
encumbrance
encyclopedia
endeavour
*enormous

enrol
enrolled
enrolment
ensure (make sure; *see* insure)
enthusiasm
enthusiastically
entirely
entrance
envelop (vb)
enveloping
envelope (for a letter)
*environment
equality
equatorial
equipped
equipment
especially
estuary, estuaries
etc. (short for et cetera)
eventual
eventually
*exaggerate
exaggeration
exceed
excessive
excel
excelling
* excellent
*except (not including; to omit; *see* accept)
exceptional
exceptionally
excite
exciting
* excitement
exclaim
exclamation
*exercise
exhaust

exhibition
*exhilarating
*existence
*expense
expensively
experience
extension
extraordinary
extraordinarily
*extravagant
extravagance
*extremely
exuberant
exuberance

facilities
factories
Fahrenheit
failure
faint (swoon; weak; *see* feint)
faithful
faithfully
fallacy
*family, families
familiar
famous
fantasies
fantastically
fascination
fastening
fatigue
fatiguing
favour
* favourite
favourable
feasible
*February
feign (pretend)
feint (sham move, pretence; *see* faint)
feminine

8

femininity
ferociously
fervour
fictitious
fidgeted
field
fierce
 fiercely
*fiery
fifth
finally
*finish
flavour
fluorescent
forbidden
 forbidding
foreboding
 (foretelling)
forecast
forecourt
foregoing
 (preceding)
forgoing (doing
 without)
*foreign
forest
forfeit
forgetting
 forgotten
 forgettable
forgivable
formally (in a
 formal way)
formerly
 (previously)
fortieth
*forty
*fourteen
fragrant
 fragrance
frantically
freight (cargo)
*friend

frightful
 frightfully
fuelling
*fulfil
* fulfilled
* fulfilment
fully
funnily
furniture
future

gaily
 gaiety
galloped
gaol (or jail)
 gaoler (or jailer)
gardening
 gardener
gas, gases
*gauge (measure;
 see gouge)
general
 generally
generous
 generosity
ghastly
ghetto
ghost
gipsy, gipsies (or
 gypsy)
giraffe
glamour
 glamorous
glasses
glimpse
glorious
gnarled
gnawing
goal (target)
goddess
gorgeous
gorilla (ape)
gossiped

gouge (scoop out;
 see gauge)
*government
governor
gracious
gradual
 gradually
graffiti (plural)
grammar
 grammatical
granary
grandeur
*grateful
 gratefully
 gratitude
greasy
 greasily
grief
* grievous
 grievance
gruesome
*guarantee
 guaranteed
 guaranteeing
guard
 guardian
guer(r)illa (raiding
 soldier)
guest
guide
 guidance
guild
guillotine
guilty
guise (manner)

half, halves
hallucination
handicapped
handkerchief
hangar (shed)
hanger (for
 clothes, etc.)

9

*happened
happily
happiness
harass
harassment
hassle
hastened
hazard
hear (listen; see
here)
heard
heaven
*height
heir
heiress
here (in this place;
see hear)
hero, heroes
hideous
hindrance
history
historically
hoard (store; see
horde)
holiday
honestly
honour
* honourable
hoofs or hooves
horde (crowd,
pack; see hoard)
horror
horrifying
horrified
horrific
horrifically
humour
* humorous
Hungary
hungry
hungrily
hygiene
hymn

*hypocrisy
hypocrite
hypocritically
hysterical (in a
frenzy)
hysterically

iceberg
icicle
identical
identically
idiosyncrasy
idle (lazy)
idol (of worship)
idyllic
illegal
illegally
illegible
(indecipherable;
see eligible)
illegibly
illicit (illegal; see
elicit)
illiterate
illiteracy
illusion (false
image; see
allusion)
imagine
imaginary
imitate
immature
*immediate
* immediately
immense
immensely
immigrant (enters
a country; see
emigrant)
imminent (near,
threatening; see
eminent)
immoral

immortal
inadequate
in between (2
words)
*incidentally
incredible
incredibly
incurred
indebted
indefinite
indefinitely
*independent
independence
indestructible
indictment
(criminal charge)
indispensable
ineligible (not fit
to be chosen)
*in fact (2 words)
inferred
infinite
infinitely
inflammable
information
*in front (2 words)
innate (inborn)
innocent
innocence
innuendo(e)s
innumerable
inoculate
inspired
*in spite of (3
words)
install
installation
instalment
insure (take out an
insurance policy;
see ensure)
insurrection
*intellectual

intelligible
intention
  intentionally
*interested
interfering
  interference
interpreted
*interrupt
intimate
  intimately
into (entering, inside)
in to (2 senses e.g. he came in to see us)
intrigue
  intriguing
introduce
invisible
involved
  involvement
iridescent
irrecoverable
irregular
  irregularly
irrelevant
  irrelevance
irreparable
irreplaceable
irresistible
irresponsibly
irreverent
irreversible
irritate
  irritably
island
isle (island)
itinerary
*its (belonging to it)
*it's (it is or it has)

jealous

jeopardy
jewellery or jewelry
  jeweller
jockeys
journey, journeys
judgment (or judgement)
juicy
  juicily
justifying
  justified

keenness
khaki
kidnapped
  kidnapper
knew (past tense of to know; see new)
knife, knives
knitting
knock-kneed
know (be aware of; see no)
  knowledge
* knowledgeable
knuckles

labelled
laboratory
labour
  laborious
lady, ladies
laid (never layed)
language
larva (insect grub; see lava)
latitude
latter (last referred to)
lava (volcanic; see larva)
lead (to guide;

metal)
led (past tense of to lead)
leant (past tense of to lean; see lent)
leapt (or leaped)
legend
  legendary
leisure
length
lent (past of to lend; see leant)
leopard
liaise
  liaison
*library, libraries
  librarian
licence (n.)
license (usually vb)
lieutenant
lightening (making lighter)
*lightning (flash)
likelihood
limited
liqueur (strong sweet drink)
liquor (any alcohol)
listening
  listener
literary
  literature
livelihood
loaf, loaves
loathe (hate)
  loathsome
loth/loath (unwilling)
lonely
* loneliness
longitude

*loose (free,
untie(d); *see* lose)
lorry, lorries
*lose (fail to win or
keep; *see* loose)
luxury
lying

magazine
magic
magnificent
magnificence
*maintenance
managing
manageable
manner (way; *see*
manor)
manoeuvre
manoeuvring
manor (house; *see*
manner)
mantelpiece
margarine
*marriage
married
marrying
marshal (officer;
arrange in order)
martial (adj. of
war, the army)
marvelled
* marvellous
massacre
mathematics
mathematician
mattress
maybe (perhaps)
may be (e.g. it may
be)
*meanness
meant
measure
mechanically

*medicine
medically
medieval or
mediaeval
Mediterranean
melancholy
merriment
messenger
metaphor(s)
meteorology
meter (measuring
box)
metre (measure of
length)
mil(e)age
mimic
mimicking
miniature
ministry,
ministries
minute (tiny and
60 secs)
miracle
miraculous
miscellaneous
mischief
* mischievous
mislaid
misshapen
misspell
moccasin
modelled
momentarily
monastery
monkey, monkeys
moral (right,
virtuous; a
lesson)
morale
(confidence)
mortgage
motto, mottoes
mountain

mountainous
moustache(s)
murderess
murderous
murky
*murmuring
muscle (in the
body)
mussel (mollusc)
mystery
mysterious
mystifying
mystified

naïve
naturally
*necessary
necessarily
* necessity
negotiate
negro, negroes
*neighbours
neither
nephew
niece
ninety
*ninth
no (not yes,
without; *see*
know)
noisy
noisily
*no one (2 words)
or no-one
*noticeable (easy to
see)
noticeably
nuclear
nuisance

obedient
obituary
obscene
obstacle

*occasion
occasional
* occasionally
occupying
occupied
occur
* occurred
* occurrence
*of (belonging, relating to)
*off (away from, down from)
offence
offensive
offer
* offered
often
old-fashioned
*omitted
omission
opened
opening
operation
opinion
*opportunity
oppose
opponent
* opposition
oral (spoken, by mouth; see aural)
ordinary
ordnance (map; guns)
original
originally
outfitters
outrageous
overall
overrule

*paid (never payed)
pamphlet
panel

panelling
panic
panicked
panic-stricken
paraffin
paragraph
*parallel
paralleled
parallelogram
paralyse
paralysis
paraphernalia
*parliament
parliamentary
particular
particularly
*passed (did pass; has passed)
*past (all other uses)
pastime
patience
patiently
patrol
patrolled
pavilion
peace (not war; quiet; see piece)
peaceful
* peacefully
peculiar
* peculiarly
pedal (foot lever)
pedalling
peddle (sell)
penicillin
perceive
perhaps
perilous
permanent
*permitted
permission
permissible

*perseverance
persistent
persistence
personal (private, individual)
personally
personnel (n. staff, employees)
perspiration
persuade
persuasion
pharmacist
phenomenon (singular)
phenomena (plural)
phenomenally
photos
phrase
physical
* physically
physics
physician
physique
pianos
Piccadilly
picnic
picnicking
picnicker
picture (painting)
picturesque
piece (part; see peace)
pierce
piercing
pigeon
pitcher (jug)
pitch, pitches
pitiful
pitifully
pitiless
plain (flat country; clear; not pretty)

13

plane (level; tool;
  tree; aircraft)
playwright
pleasant
plebeian
pneumatic
pneumonia
poisonous
police
pony, ponies
popular
Portuguese
possess
* possession
potato, potatoes
*practice (n.)
*practise (vb)
pray (worship; see
  prey)
precede (go
  before; see
  proceed)
predator
predecessor
*preferred
  preference
*prejudice
premier
prepare
* preparation
prescription
  (order, e.g. a
  doctor's)
presence
pretence
  pretension
  pretentious
prettily
prevail
  prevalent
previous
prey (hunted
  creature; see

pray)
priest
primary
  primarily
primeval
*primitive
princess,
  princesses
*principal (chief;
  leader)
*principle (rule,
  law, code of
  conduct)
*privilege
*probably
*procedure
*proceed (go along;
  see precede)
  procession
  proclamation
*profess
  profession
  professionally
* professor
proficient
profited
program (for a
  computer)
programme
pronunciation
proofs
propaganda
propel
  propelling
  propeller
*prophecy,
  prophecies (n.)
*prophesy (vb)
  prophesying
  prophesied
prophet
  (forecaster)
proscription

(banning)
protein
protrude
prove
psalm
psychiatrist
psychology
  psychologically
*publicly
pulley, pulleys
punctuation
*pursue
  pursuing
  pursuit
pyjamas
pyramid

quality
*quarrel
* quarrelled
*quarter
quay (wharf)
queue
  queuing
  queued
quiet (silent)
quite (fairly; very;
  completely)

rain (water; see
  reign, rein)
raise (lift; make
  grow; see rase)
rarely
  rarity
  rarefied
rase/raze
  (demolish)
realise
  realistically
* really
reassurance
recede

14

recession
*receive
* receipt
recipe, recipes
*recognise or
    recognize
*recommend
reconnaissance
    reconnoitre
recover (regain
    health or
    possession)
re-cover (cover
    again)
recurring
    recurrence
*referring
    reference
    referee
reform (correct,
    improve)
re-form (form
    again)
refrigerator (or
    fridge)
regretted
    regrettable
regularly
reign (rule; *see*
    rain)
rein(s) (strap)
*relevant
    relevance
relief
    relieved
religion
* religious
remembrance
reminiscence
Renaissance or
    Renascence
renowned
repel

repelling
repellent
repetition
    repetitive
resemble
    resemblance
reservoir
resign (give up)
re-sign (sign
    again)
resistance
responsible
    responsibility
restaurant
retrieve
revealed
review (survey)
revue (stage show)
rheumatism
rhinoceros
rhyme
*rhythm
ridicule
*ridiculous
right (not left;
    correct; just
    claim; *see* rite)
    righteous
rigorous
rite (religious
    ceremony; *see*
    right)
riveting
rogue (villain)
role (actor's part;
    person's job)
roll (all other
    senses)
roof, roofs
rouge (on cheeks)
rout (defeat)
route (direction)
    routeing

routine

sacrilege
    sacrilegious
safely
    safety
said (past of say)
sandal
satellite
Saturday
scandal
scarcely
    scarcity
*scene
    scenery
    scenically
schedule
scheme
school
    scholar
    scholastic
*science
    scientifically
scissors
scream
screech
seam (edge, layer;
    see seem)
secondary
secrecy
*secretary
seem (appear; *see*
    seam)
*seize
sense
*sentence
*separate
    separation
sergeant or
    serjeant
series
    serial (story in
    parts; *see* cereal)

serviceable
severely
sew(n) (with a needle; see sow(n))
shear (shave)
sheer (all other senses)
sheik(h) (e.g. of Arabia)
shelf, shelves
shepherd
sheriff
shield
shining (sun)
shinning (up a tree)
shriek
shyer
  shyly
  shyness
siege
sieve
sight (thing seen; vision; see site)
signalled
silhouette
*similarly
  similarity
simile, similes
simultaneous
sincere
* sincerely
  sincerity
singeing (burning)
site (place; position; see sight)
skein (of wool)
ski-ing
*skilful
* skilfully
slanderous

slyer
  slyly
  slyness
soldier
solemn
  solemnly
solicit
  solicitor
soliloquy, soliloquies
somersault or summersault
sorrowful
  sorrowfully
souvenirs
sovereign
  sovereignty
sow(n) (seeds; see sew(n))
spacious
speak
* speech
specially
species
specific
spectre
sphere
splendour
sponsor
spoonful(s)
sprightly
squalor
  squalid
squawk
stationary (still)
stationery (envelopes, etc.)
  stationer's
statistics
  statistically
  statistician
stile (steps; see style)

stomach
straight (direct; not bent)
straits (narrow places, difficulties)
strength
*stubbornness
style (fashion, manner; see stile)
subtle
* subtly
  subtlety
*succeed
  success
* successful
  successfully
  successor
succumb
suddenness
suffering
suggestion
suit (fit; of clothes, cards, etc.)
suite (of furniture, rooms)
superintendent
*supersede
supervise
  supervisor
supposed
suppression
sure (certain)
  surely
surfeit
*surprise
surround
surveyor
survivors
susceptible
suspense
swingeing (cuts)
syllabus

16

symmetry
symmetrically
sympathy
sympathetically
symphony

talent
tariff
tattoo(s)
taught (past tense
of to teach)
taut (tight)
*technique
technical
* technically
temperamental
temperature
*temporary
temporarily
tenant
tendency
terrify
terrific
* terrifically
terrible
theatre
*their (belonging to
them)
*there (in that
place; there is,
there are . . .)
*they're (they are)
*theirs (something
belonging to
them)
*there's (there is or
there has)
thief, thieves
*thorough
threshold
threw (past tense
of to throw)
through (by or

from one end to
another)
tidily
tidiness
tier (row)
tire (weary; *see*
tyre)
tiring
*to (towards; to do,
to play, etc.; *see*
too)
tobacco
tobogganing
tomato, tomatoes
tomorrow (1
word)
tongue
*too (excessively;
also; *see* to)
torpedo,
torpedoes
tractor
traffic
trafficking
*tragedy
tragic
tragically
tranquil
tranquillity
transferred
transmitted
travel
travelled
traveller
treachery
*truly
truthfully
trying
tried
Tuesday
tussle
*twelfth
tying (a knot)

typical
typically
*tyranny
tyrannical
tyre (e.g. on a car;
see tire)

ultimately
uncontrolled
uncontrollable
*unconscious
underrate
*undoubtedly
universities
unnamed
*unnatural
*unnecessary
unnecessarily
unnoticed
unsuccessful
until (or till)
usually

vaccinate
vacuum
valley(s)
valuable
* valuably
vapour
vaporise
various
variety
*vegetable
vehicle
veil
vein (of blood,
streak)
vendor
vengeance
vertical
vertically
veterinary
veto, vetoes
*vicious (cruel)

17

*view
vigour
vigorous
*villain
visible
visited
* visitor
volcano, volcanoes
volley(s)
volunteered
voluntary
voluntarily

waist (part of the body; see waste)
waive (forgo, not claim; see wave)
wander (stray about; see wonder)
warily
waste (rubbish, barren land; see waist)
wave (shake; sea motion; see waive)
wearily
weariness
weather (climate; see whether)

Wednesday
weigh
weight
weir (in a river)
*weird
welcome
welfare
were (past of are)
we're (we are)
where (in what place)
whereas (1 word)
whether (if; see weather)
whiff
whisper
whistle
whole
* wholly
*who's (who is or who has)
*whose (belonging to whom)
wife, wives
wilful
wilfully
wintry
wiry
wisdom
wisely
wisp

witch, witches
*withhold
withheld
witticism
wittily
woman, women
wonder (marvel, doubt; astonishment; see wander)
*woollen
*worshipped
wreak (vengeance)
wrecked
wrench
writhing
writing
written

yacht
yield
yoke (of a plough; burden)
yolk (of an egg)
your (belonging to you)
you're (you are)
yourselves

3

Diagnose your spelling problems

This chapter is designed to help you isolate and then remedy your weaknesses. Each test contains thirty spellings. Answers are in chapter 14. If you make more than three mistakes in a test, you should study the chapter(s) referred to at the end of the test. (Try these tests again later after you have studied the whole book.)

1 Choose the right word from the following. Write out each sentence.

  (a) We don't *no/know were/where/we're*
      were/where/we're going.
  (b) Are *there/their/they're* friends *there/their/they're*
      to/too/two?
  (c) *Theirs/there's* no doubt that it is *past/passed* her bedtime.
  (d) I wonder *who's/whose* car that is and *who's/whose*
      parked it like that.
  (e) Is this *your/you're* doing? Look what *your/you're* doing!
  (f) It is far *to/too/two* hot *to/too/two* go *to/too/two* the
      cinema.
  (g) A piece *of/off/have* slate must *of/off/have* fallen
      of/off/have the roof.
  (h) Illness didn't seem to have any *affect/effect* on her
      performance since she was still first *past/passed* the
      winning post.
  (i) *Lets/let's* consider the *principal/principle* arguments in
      his speech.
  (j) They will all *accept/except* the invitation *accept/except*
      John.
  (k) The fox was *quiet/quite quiet/quite*, hoping
      to *loose/lose* its pursuers by *laying/lying* low under the
      bracken.

(l) He *laid/lay* there for hours before anyone noticed him.

(m) Do you need spelling *practice/practise*?

(*Answers in chapter 14. See chapter 4.*)

2 Write out the plural form of each of these, e.g. book (singular) becomes books (plural):

lady	thief	ox	dinghy
valley	business	spoonful	bus
wife	chimney	factory	potato
ally	volley	phenomenon	passer-by
hero	pony	veto	cargo
criterion	roof	shelf	lorry
crisis	child	simile	
chief	sheep	echo	

(*Answers in chapter 14. See chapter 5.*)

3 All of these are misspelt. Write out each word correctly:

misscheivious	medecine	vegtabul	Febuery
intressting	burguler	goverment	undoubtably
genraly	interlectuall	rediculus	envollved
supprize	centuary	sepperate	twelth
secertery	laboretery	littrature	disscription
perculierlly	liberary	terificly	primmative
hypocracy	mathmaticks	infrount	
deffinatley	contempory	reckonize	

(*Answers in chapter 14. See chapters 7 and 8.*)

4 Insert 'ie' or 'ei' in each of these:

ach—ve	conc—t	w—rd	retr—ve
bel—f	rec—ve	h—ght	hyg—ne
dec—t	s—ve	fr—ndly	rel—f
bes—ge	n—ghbour	prot—n	c—ling
s—ze	sover—gn	fr—ght	br—fly
perc—ve	counterf—t	h—rloom	gr—vance
handkerch—f	f—ndish	n—ce	
w—gh	spec—s	p—ce	

(*Answers in chapter 14. See chapter 7.*)

5 All of these are misspelt. Write out each word correctly:

definnate	interuptian	antedote	aknollege
drunkeness	disatissfied	exitement	imediate
dissappoint	dissapear	procede	oponnent

unaturel	overule	sucsede	comottion
stuborness	carefull	acellerate	iregulierly
witheld	enviroment	forcourt	aquire
wellfare	disimiler	ilegable	
skillfull	fulfill	comited	

(Answers in chapter 14. See chapter 8.)

6 Form adverbs ending in '-ly' from each of these, making any other necessary changes (e.g. quick becomes quickly):

exceptional	fantastic	extraordinary	peculiar
drastic	public	incidental	occasional
beautiful	true	cool	immediate
accidental	careful	sincere	invaluable
hungry	full	faithful	pathetic
humble	probable	tragic	successful
real	unnecessary	subtle	
similar	frantic	whole	

(Answers in chapter 14. See chapter 10.)

7 (a) Add '-ed' to each of these, making any other necessary changes (e.g. climb becomes climbed):

supply   carry   dry   pity   survey   enjoy   copy convey

(b) Add '-ing' to each of these, making any other necessary changes:

marry   survey   supply   tie   dye   deny   delay try   lie   singe

(c) Add '-ness' to each of these, making any other necessary changes:

lonely   lively   pretty   tidy

(d) Add '-est' to each of these, making any other necessary changes:

shy   pretty   lonely   likely   sly   gay   busy hungry

(Answers in chapter 14. See chapter 9.)

8 (a) Add '-ing' to each of these, making any other necessary changes:

care   forgive   canoe   queue   pine   mimic slope   argue   manoeuvre   achieve   die   picnic like   pursue   come   notice   admire   manage re-route

(b) Add '-ment' to each of these, making any other necessary changes:

achieve   argue   encourage

(c) Add '-able' to each of these, making any other necessary changes:

believe   notice   change   forgive

(d) Add '-ly' to each of these, making any other necessary changes:

due   lone   immense   true

(*Answers in chapter 14. See chapters 9 and 10.*)

9 (a) Form adjectives ending in '-ous' from each of these (e.g. calamity becomes calamitous):

courage   glamour   advantage   labour   slander
mystery   grace   fury   humour   outrage   vigour
religion   marvel   disaster   luxury

(b) Form adjectives ending in '-able' or '-ible' from each of these (e.g. return becomes returnable). Make any other necessary changes:

service   practice   knowledge   agree   permit
value   change   divide   collapse   honour

(c) Add '-ent' or '-ant' to each of these:

extravag——   signific——   eleg——   neglig——
magnific——

(*Answers in chapter 14. See chapter 11.*)

10 Add '-ing' to each of these, making any other necessary changes:

swim	occur	begin	quarrel
scare	regret	dine	conceal
profit	refer	prefer	parallel
fit	emit	admit	gallop
defer	develop	transfer	kidnap
benefit	propel	rivet	pocket
commit	cancel	omit	
offer	worship	murmur	

(*Answers in chapter 14. See chapter 9.*)

22

4

Words often confused

Many common errors are caused by the confusing of
words which sound alike and by uncertainty over punctuation. The following should be recognised as possible
danger spots and checked carefully.

its and it's

its means belonging to it. e.g. The horse had hurt its leg and was not
at its best.
it's is short for it is (or it has). e.g. It's lame. It's limping. It's fallen.

your and you're

your means belonging to you. e.g. This is your life. I don't like your
leaving early.
you're is short for you are. e.g. You're looking well. You're leaving
early.

theirs and there's

theirs means something belonging to them. e.g. Theirs is the red
van. That is theirs, not ours.
there's is short for there is (or there has). e.g. There's no chance of
rain. There's been no rain for weeks.

their, there and they're

their means belonging to them. e.g. They lost their boots in the
mud.
there means in that place (compare here and where) and is used in
impersonal forms like there is and there are, there will be and
there were. e.g. Look there. There is and there can be only one
solution.

they're is short for they are. e.g. They're not at home. They're coming round the corner.

who's and whose

who's is short for who is (and who has). e.g. Who's there? Who's borrowed my pen? The girl who's coming to tea is a student of mine.

whose means belonging to whom. e.g. Whose book is that? That is the boy whose sister has had an accident.

where, were and we're

where means in or to which place (and rhymes with there). e.g. Where are you going? I don't know where I'm going.

were is the past tense of 'are' (and rhymes with fur). e.g. They were in Paris when you were. We were waiting patiently.

we're is short for we are (and rhymes with ear). e.g. We're not sure what we're doing.

lets and let's

lets is the verb form used with he, she or it. e.g. I hope he lets us go.

let's is short for let us. e.g. Let's all go down the Strand.

one's and ones

one's means belonging to one. e.g. One must mind one's Ps and Qs. (It can also be short for one is (or one has). e.g. One's no idea when one's going to die.)

ones is the plural of one. e.g. Which ones do you prefer? I want the ones in the window.

of, off and have

of is pronounced 'ov' and means belonging to, coming from, relating to, by ... e.g. Of course I like the poetry of Thomas Hardy. He is a favourite of mine.

off means away from or down from a place. e.g. He fell off the cliff. He knocked the cup off the table.

have is a verb, used to form the past tenses of many verbs. (It can be abbreviated as in we've for we have). e.g. I must have made a mistake. I should have checked more carefully.

to, too and two

to means towards and is also used to form the verb infinitive (e.g. to play, to sing, to eat). e.g. I went to the seaside. I hoped to catch prawns. To see is to believe.

too means excessively and also. e.g. It was too hot. I was late, too.

two is the number. e.g. The two men fought a duel.

lose and loose

lose means fail to win or fail to keep. (It rhymes with whose.) e.g. He happened to lose his shoe but didn't lose the race.

loose means free or untied and to set free. (It rhymes with noose.) e.g. His shoe-lace was too loose.

passed and past

passed is a verb, both in its past tense and its past participle. It has various meanings:
- as past tense: e.g. He passed me the ball. He passed me in the street. He passed his exams. Time passed slowly.
- as past participle: e.g. He has passed his exams. He had passed the line before he fell. The time has passed very quickly.

past is used for all other parts of speech and meanings:
- as a noun: e.g. Archaeologists are interested in the past.
- as an adjective: e.g. Past civilisations are interesting. The hour is past.
- as an adverb: e.g. The lorries hurtled past.
- as a preposition: e.g. He ran past us. He ran past the winning post. It is past midnight.

lie and lay

lie means to put yourself in a horizontal position.

Its present tenses are: I lie, I am lying...

Its past tenses are: I lay, I was lying,

    I have/had lain...

e.g. As I was tired I lay down for a while.

lay means to place something else (like a plate, a book or an egg) down flat.

Its present tenses are: I lay it, I am laying it down...

Its past tenses are: I laid it, I was laying it down...
I have/had laid it down...
e.g. I laid my book on the table that my mother was still laying.

affect and effect

affect is a verb meaning to influence or produce a change in something. e.g. Smoking can affect your health.

effect is a noun meaning result (or operation). e.g. The effect of his words was amazing. They put their plan into effect. (Effect can also be a verb meaning to bring something about. e.g. He effected his escape with ease.)

principal and principle

principal means leading, most important. It can be an adjective (e.g. Barcelona is one of the principal cities in Spain.) or a noun (e.g. He asked the Principal of the college to act as his referee.).

principle means a basic law or truth, or a rule of right behaviour. e.g. Have you forgotten Archimedes' principle? It's the principle of the thing that counts.

practice and practise: prophecy and prophesy

The noun has 'c', the verb 's'.* Remember advice and device (nouns) and to advise and to devise (verbs), which are pronounced differently.

practice (noun): e.g. a piano practice; the doctor's practice; practice makes perfect.

practise (verb): e.g. He needs to practise his spelling. He would practise it every day.

prophecy (noun; the end is pronounced 'see'): e.g. He was amazed when the prophecy came true.

prophesy (verb; the end is pronounced 'eye'): Fortune-tellers would prophesy disasters at the sun's eclipse.

accept and except

accept is a verb meaning to receive. e.g. I accept your kind offer of help.

* In American English both the noun and verb are spelt with a 'c'.

except is a preposition meaning not including. e.g. All except one were drowned. (Except can also be a verb meaning to omit or exclude. e.g. I hope you will except him from your list of suspects. Compare 'present company excepted'.)

Verbs sometimes confused:

choose (rhymes with whose) is the present tense and the infinitive form (to choose).
chose (rhymes with nose) is the past tense.
e.g. I choose the same cake today as I chose yesterday.

lead (rhymes with bead) is the present tense. (The noun lead, which rhymes with bed, is the metal.)
led (rhymes with bed) is the past tense.
e.g. We lead the same life today as we have always led.

leant is the past tense of to lean.
lent is the past tense of to lend.
e.g. As he leant on the table, I asked him if he still had the book I had lent him.

flowed is the past tense of to flow (water).
flown is the past participle of to fly (birds).
e.g. The water flowed sweetly by, but the birds had flown away.

sew(n) – i.e. with a needle
sow(n) – i.e. seeds
e.g. I'll sew the button on while you sow the lettuce seeds.

Check for 'howlers' or 'slips of the pen' in the following:

no – not any, not yes
know – (verb) to be aware of
e.g. I know you had no part in it.

new – not old
knew – past tense of to know
e.g. He knew that she would buy a new coat.

hear – listen
here – in this place
e.g. I hear that the Queen was here today.

weather – rain, wind, sunshine, etc.
whether – if
e.g. We shall go whether the weather is fine or not.

peace – quiet, opposite of war
piece – part
e.g. There was an uneasy peace after a war had been fought over a piece of useless land.

threw – past tense of to throw
through – by or from one end or side to the other
e.g. He threw the stone through the window.

quiet – silent
quite – fairly, very, completely
e.g. The house was quite quiet.

aloud – out loud
allowed – permitted
e.g. You are not allowed to think aloud in the examination room.

break(s) – smash(es), rip(s); intervals
brake(s) – stop(s), put(s) on the brakes of a car, etc.
e.g. If you brake too hard on this bicycle you might break your neck.

Note See the check-list in chapter 2 for more words commonly confused.

Test yourself (Cover the rest of the page when tackling this test.)

1 Choose the correct word:
Whose/who's is it? *Its/it's* mine. *Lets/let's* see. *Their/there/they're* you are then. But *your/you're* cheating. *There's/theirs* nothing *their/there/they're*. *Where/were/we're* did you hide it? I don't *know/no*. It must *of/off/have* slipped *through/threw* my fingers.

2 Insert their, there or they're:
————— is no doubt that ————— singing is not what ————— famous for.

3 Insert past or passed: He had already gone ————— me before he ————— me the ball.

4 Insert lose or loose: This tooth is so ————— that I shall probably ————— it.

5 Insert lets or let's: If he ————— us then ————— do it.

6 Insert to, too or two: There were ————— many for all of us ————— have a game.

28

7 Insert accept or except: They agreed to ———— all the entries ———— mine.

8 Insert practice or practise: We all need to ———— our spelling.

9 Insert lying or laying in the first space and laid or lain in the other two: Yesterday he was ———— in the bed where he had ———— for the last two weeks, but today the nurses have ———— him on a sunbed outside.

10 Insert principal or principle: His ———— concern was for the legal ———— involved in the case.

(Answers in chapter 14.)

5

Punctuation and plurals

THE APOSTROPHE

The apostrophe has two main uses:

1 To show possession in nouns.

The singular noun takes an apostrophe then an 's'.
e.g. that lady's hat, a man's shoe.

Plurals ending in 's' add the apostrophe after the final 's'.
e.g. those ladies' hats.

Be careful with plurals which do not end in 's', like men, children.
e.g. men's shoes, children's games.

In the Middle Ages the possessive form was shown by an 'es' ending as in The Knygh*tes* Tale by Chaucer. The apostrophe was later introduced to mark the omission of this 'e'.

Note Do not confuse simple noun plurals, which should have *no* apostrophe, with the singular and plural *possessive* forms: e.g. That lady's hat is ugly. Those ladies' hats are ugly. Those ladies (i.e. a simple plural) are wearing ugly hats.

(It is wrong for the greengrocer to write 'apple's, pear's and plum's'; it should be 'apples, pears and plums'.)

(The only time the apostrophe can be used for plural forms is with non-words like figures and letters: e.g. Dot your i's and cross your t's – this prevents confusion between i's and is.)

Do *not* put apostrophes in the following: ours, yours, theirs, and its when it means belonging to it. These are not *nouns*. (The only exception is one's, meaning belonging to one.)

2 To indicate a contraction.

The apostrophe is placed where the letter(s) has (have) been omitted.

e.g.
I'll – I will/shall
I'd – I would/should
can't – cannot
doesn't – does not
aren't – are not

we're – we are
you're – you are
they're – they are
there's – there is (or has)
it's – it is (or it has)

Note: won't – will not (originally shortened from 'wol nat')
shan't – shall not (originally abbreviated as 'sha'n't')

ONE WORD OR MORE?

1 The following are two or more words:

They should not be written as one:

in front (2)
in fact (2)
in between (2)
in spite of (3)

a lot of (3)
as well (2)
no one (2) (or no-one)

2 The following are single words:

although
tomorrow (or to-morrow)
straightforward (when it means simple or honest)
whereas

3 Note the difference between the following:

already – by now e.g. I already know this.
all ready – all are ready e.g. Are you all ready?

altogether – completely e.g. I do not altogether understand you.
all together – all in one place e.g. I have put these words all together.

always – ever, constantly e.g. I always check carefully.
all ways – all methods or ways e.g. All ways are closed.

maybe – perhaps e.g. Maybe I shall go; maybe not.
may be – two verbs e.g. It may be fine tomorrow.

into – inside, entering e.g. He went into the room.
in to – two separate senses e.g. He came in to tell us the news.

anyone, anybody, someone, somebody, everyone, everybody, nobody, anything, something, everything, nothing, sometime and sometimes, all express a *single* idea: any one, every one, etc. mean any single one, every single one, etc. The two words express separate ideas and are often pronounced with the stress on the second word.

HYPHENS

The hyphen is used when attaching a prefix to form a (new) compound word, and especially when confusion might result, as with resign and re-sign.
e.g. anti-nuclear

It is used, too, when a compound is formed from two or more other words.
e.g. a devil-may-care attitude

(There is a natural tendency for well-used hyphenations to become single words.
e.g. multi-storey becomes multistorey.)

CAPITAL LETTERS

Apart from its use at the beginning of sentences and passages of direct speech, the capital letter is also used:
- for proper nouns (i.e. names of *particular* persons, places, things) and for months of the year and days of the week
  e.g. Jane, Michael, Liverpool, England, Fahrenheit, Piccadilly, February, Wednesday, Saturday, Mediterranean, Arctic Ocean
- for adjectives derived from proper nouns, especially places and people
  e.g. English, Victorian, Christian, Caribbean, Portuguese
  (except for common phrases where the original meaning has been lost, e.g. french windows, venetian blinds, brussels sprouts)
- for the first and all main words in *any* kind of title
  e.g. *Far from the Madding Crowd*, *Panorama*, *The Times*, The United Nations
- for the pronoun I
- for He, Him, His when referring to God, and when a noun is

personified (like Father Time) or considered as a grand abstract idea

e.g. He worshipped Beauty.

PLURALS

The general rule is to add an 's', or, after s, x, z, ch, sh (sibilants), to add 'es'.

e.g. boy – boys   bus – buses   box – boxes   fez – fezes
sandwich – sandwiches   wish – wishes

Nouns ending in 'y'

- If the noun ends in a *consonant* followed by a 'y', *drop* the 'y' and add *'ies'*

  e.g. lady – ladies   pony – ponies   lorry – lorries
  monastery – monasteries   ministry – ministries
  ally – allies

- If there is a *vowel* immediately before the 'y', *simply add 's'*

  e.g. donkey – donkeys   valley – valleys   chimney – chimneys   survey – surveys   alley – alleys

Nouns ending in 'o'

Except for those listed below, simply add 's'.

The '-os' plural is used for words of Italian origin like musical terms

e.g. pianos, sopranos and for shortened words like photos, biros, videos.

Exceptions: potato – potatoes   tomato – tomatoes   cargo – cargoes   negro – negroes   echo – echoes   hero – heroes
veto – vetoes   mottoes   volcanoes   mosquitoes   embargoes

Nouns ending in '-fe' and 'f'

There is no rule, though the pronunciation is usually a clear guide:

wife – wives   knife – knives   loaf – loaves   half – halves
thief – thieves   shelf – shelves   self – selves   leaf – leaves
wolf – wolves

Note: chief – chiefs;   roof – roofs

(Some have either: e.g. hoofs or hooves, scarfs or scarves, wharfs or wharves, turfs or turves, handkerchiefs or handkerchieves.)

Foreign words

Some words keep their foreign plurals, especially those from the Greek, ending in '-sis' and '-on':

e.g. crisis – crises   oasis – oases   criterion – criteria
    phenomenon – phenomena
Also: from Latin: larva – larvae   stimulus – stimuli   cactus –
                cacti   medium – media (mediums for ghosts)
       from French: bureau – bureaux (or bureaus)

Hyphenated words

These usually add the 's' to the main noun part, e.g. passers-by, sons-in-law. (Those formed from verbs which have adverbs attached to them take an 's' at the end, e.g. lay-offs, lay-bys.)

Words having the same form in singular and plural

e.g. sheep, aircraft, series.

Test yourself (Cover the above when tackling this test.)

1 Write these sentences out correctly:

Our local stationers seems to sell alotof christmas gift's and chil-
drens games, where as your's dosent.
Inspiteof all the english teams efforts to re-cover their lost form,
noone managed to score, all though the team was playing infront of
a home crowd.
The womens institute has, infact, all ready held it's annual meeting.

2 Form plurals from each of these:

basis   tomato   journey   tax   piccolo   volley   ache
folly   laboratory   roof   storey   send-off

Put both nouns into the plural form (e.g. the boy's book becomes
the boys' books): the ship's cargo   the thief's knife   the witch's
prophecy   the child's pony

(Answers in chapter 14.)

6

A brief history of English spelling

(Chapters 6, 7 and 8, studied together, will give you a better understanding of English spelling by digging down to its roots.)

English spelling is the product of a mixture of different languages and the overlapping of one spelling system on another. Many apparent oddities in our spelling are due to changes in pronunciation since the Middle Ages – sometimes the early spelling has been kept even though the pronunciation of the word has changed; sometimes the spelling has been changed while the pronunciation, at least temporarily, has remained the same.

The Old English 'hard' 'h' sound was re-spelt 'gh' by the Normans who had no such sound in French, and in the Middle Ages it was still pronounced as a 'kh' sound: hence words like night, bough, ought, high, slaughter, laughter, all of which are from Old English. The 'k' in know and knot, the 'g' in gnaw and gnarled, and the 'l' in folk and calm used to be pronounced. The 'wh' in words like where, when and white was formerly pronounced with two blowing sounds and originally spelt 'hw' as in Old English 'hwit' for white. The silent 'e', too, used to be sounded until after the fourteenth century. (Chaucer's 'Knyghtes Tale', therefore, would be pronounced with every letter sounded as 'knikhtas taala'.)

By the end of the tenth century, Old English spelling had become fairly standardised and had a logical, phonetic spelling system. Norman French imposed its own spelling system, however, as well as softening the pronunciation of 'hard' 'g' and 'k' letters. Norman scribes, who were also influenced by their knowledge of Latin, changed the spelling of Old English words to suit the French (or Latin), as well as bringing in French words with their French spelling:

thus the Old English words 'cwic' and 'cwen' were re-spelt quick and queen, and words like quit and question were introduced; the 'o' replaced an earlier 'u' to make our spelling of come and honey and tongue. (This was done to avoid confusion when 'u' came next to 'm' or 'n'.) The 'hard' 'gu' of French spelling was used in words like guard and guise, and words like honour and heir, which retain their silent 'h' as in French, came in. Like the earlier Norman scribes, Caxton's late fifteenth-century printers spelt according to their knowledge of Latin and French, though some, who were Dutch, re-spelt old words like 'gost' as ghost.

Later, Renaissance scholars revised earlier spelling to show the Latin 'root' of a word, as with corpse (from Middle English 'cors') and describe (from 'descryve'). In his dictionary of 1582 Richard Mulcaster used the now silent 'e' in words like stone and name to indicate that the vowel sound was 'long'. Sixteenth-century scholars, when introducing new words (usually from Latin, Greek or Italian), sometimes kept the Latinate spelling, as with the 'ph' in physical ('ph' being the Latin spelling of the Greek letter). Spelling of early English words was often re-modelled according to Latin: thus a 'b' was put in the Middle English words 'doute' and 'dette' to produce doubt and debt and show their origins in the Latin words dubitum and debitum. (In his famous dictionary of 1755 Dr Johnson similarly inserted a 'p' in receipt, but, illogically, failed to do so in deceit.)

By the mid-seventeenth century, English spelling had become fixed more or less as it is today, though the old 'long' 's' wasn't written as it is now until the mid-eighteenth century and there were often wide differences between private and printed spelling. Even today, in fact, variant spellings exist, like gaol/jail, grey/gray, and the '-ise'/'-ize' endings.

To conclude this brief survey of a vast subject, just a few words on American spelling and spelling reform. In his *An American Dictionary of the English Language* (1828), Noah Webster chose the variant spellings 'color' and 'center' (as well as 'defense'). He also made no exception for words ending in 'l' when applying the rule about doubling or not doubling the final consonant before vowel-suffixes (see chapter 9).

Further slight changes in spelling have resulted from the practices of the large publishing houses and newspapers, e.g. in the dropping of diphthongs in words like medieval (formerly mediæval and still sometimes seen as mediaeval). Attempts to simplify our spelling in more drastic ways, for example Bernard Shaw's phonetic spelling system with a new alphabet of forty letters, have, so far, failed.

36

TIME CHART

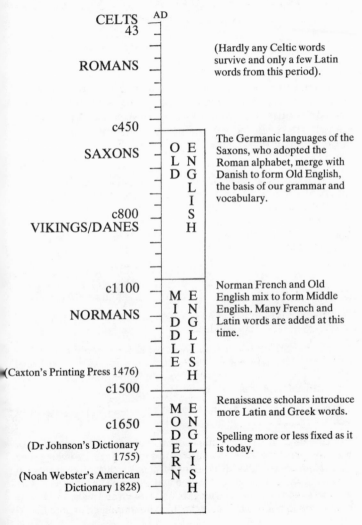

CELTS | AD
43

ROMANS

(Hardly any Celtic words survive and only a few Latin words from this period).

c450

SAXONS

O L D   E N G L I S H

The Germanic languages of the Saxons, who adopted the Roman alphabet, merge with Danish to form Old English, the basis of our grammar and vocabulary.

c800
VIKINGS/DANES

c1100

NORMANS

M I D D L E   E N G L I S H

Norman French and Old English mix to form Middle English. Many French and Latin words are added at this time.

(Caxton's Printing Press 1476)
c1500

M O D E R N   E N G L I S H

Renaissance scholars introduce more Latin and Greek words.

c1650

(Dr Johnson's Dictionary 1755)

Spelling more or less fixed as it is today.

(Noah Webster's American Dictionary 1828)

7

Pronunciation and spelling

Because English incorporates the spelling methods of several different languages (see chapter 6), we have to accustom ourselves to many variations in the way certain sounds are spelt. (Study the key to pronunciation used in your dictionary.)

CONSONANTS

The 'f' sound is represented by 'f' in refer and profited, but by 'ff' in differ and tariff, by 'gh' in tough and laughter, and by 'ph' in physics and pamphlet.

The 'k' sound is 'k' in ankle, 'kh' in khaki, 'c' in caricature and picnic, 'ck' in panicked and pocketed, 'cc' in occasion and accustom (see chapter 8), 'ch' in character and chaos, 'qu' in quay and antique.

The 's' sound is 's' in sense and series, 'c' in receive and ceiling, 'ss' in possess and assassinate, and 'sc' in scissors and scene.

The 'sh' sound appears as 'sh' in shake and shuffle but as 'ch' in chivalry and chauvinism, 'ss' in session and procession, 'ti' in commotion and promotion, 'si' in pretension and dimension, 'ci' in vicious and artificial, and even as 'sch' in schedule.

The sound 'sk' can be 'sk' in skein, 'sc' in scandal and sceptical, and 'sch' in scheme and scholar.

Because of changes in pronunciation, too, some consonants have become silent: the 'b' is no longer heard in dumb and bombing, nor the 'ch' in yacht. The 'd' is silent in handkerchief, like the 'g' in campaign and sovereignty, gnashed and gnome. The 'gh' has lost its original sound in bough and neighbour, through and night. We follow the French in not pronouncing the 'h' in honour and heir, and the 'k' is now quiet in knock-kneed knaves and their knives. The 'l' is mute in yolk and qualm and the 'n' in solemn, autumn and condemn (though it can still be heard in solemnity, autumnal and condemnation). The 'p' is seen but not heard in pneumatic, psychology, ptarmigan and raspberry, as is the 't' in the French-derived ricocheted.

And if this were not enough, the Latinisation of our spelling has inserted silent letters where they were never heard, as in debt and doubt, receipt and indictment.

THE 'HARD' AND 'SOFT' 'C' AND 'G'

When followed by an 'e' or an 'i' (or 'y'), 'c' and 'g' tend to be pronounced 'soft' (i.e. like 's' and 'j') as in Cecil and George, cylinder and gymnasium. Before the vowels 'a', 'o' and 'u' they are usually 'hard', as in catgut.

(a) To keep the 'c' and 'g' soft when adding suffixes beginning with 'a', 'o' or 'u' the silent 'e' must remain:

e.g. manageable   noticeable   knowledgeable
(Contrast navigable and practicable.)
courageous   advantageous   outrageous

(b) A 'k' is needed to keep the 'c' hard when adding suffixes beginning with 'e' or 'i', like '-ed' and '-ing':

e.g. mimic – mimicked   panic – panicked   bivouac – bivouacked   picnic – picnicking   traffic – trafficked, trafficker
(Until the nineteenth century words like panic and music had a 'k' at the end.)

(c) Sometimes a 'u' is present after a 'g' to keep it hard:

e.g. guilt   guest   guillotine   vogue   disguise
(Contrast colleague and college, league and allege.)

VOWELS

The spelling and pronunciation of English vowel sounds is, at least for the foreign student learning English, a source of dismay and confusion. Again, the apparent chaos is due to changes that have taken place in pronunciation and to the variety of spelling systems we use. (One result of this is the large number of homophones whose sense is distinguished by their spelling. See chapter 4.)

Thus, the 'ee' sound can be spelt ee, ea, ie, ei and e + consonant + e, as in meet, meat and mete (measure out); piece and peace; sealing and ceiling. (It is even ae in aegis.)

The 'ay' sound is spelt a + consonant + e or ai (as in pane and pain), or ey or ay (as in prey and pray).

The 'air' sound can be ear, a + consonant + e, air, eir, or aer, as in pear, pare (nails), pair, heir, hair, their and aerodrome.

The 'aw' sound is in pore and paw (and some pronunciations of poor), as well as in maul and dinosaur. You can hear the 'ear' sound in here and hear and pier and peer.

There is an 'oh' sound in loan and lone as well as thrown and throne; 'ah' is in father and farther, balmy and barmy. The long 'i' appears in I, find, aisle, height, high and fiery; the long 'u' in cue, queue, few, feud and you. And, confusion's masterpiece, the spelling 'ough' can be pronounced 'uff' and 'ow', 'off' and 'oo', 'uh' and even 'up', as in rough, bough, cough, through, thorough and hiccough.

> I take it you already know
> Of tough and bough and cough and dough?
> Others may stumble but not you
> On hiccough, thorough, lough and through.
> Well done! And now you wish perhaps
> To learn the less familiar traps.
>
> Beware of heard, a dreadful word,
> That looks like beard and sounds like bird;
> And dead, it's said like bed not bead –
> For goodness' sake don't call it deed!
> Watch out for meat and great and threat
> (They rhyme with suite and straight and debt).
>
> A moth is not a moth in mother,
> Nor both in bother, broth in brother;
> And here is not a match for there,
> Nor dear and fear for bear and pear,
> And then there's dose and rose and lose –
> Just look at them – and goose and choose;

And cork and work and card and ward,
And font and front, and word and sword,
And do and go and thwart and cart –
A dreadful language? Man alive,
I'd mastered it when I was five.

(Herbert Farjeon)

THE 'EE' SOUND: 'IE' OR 'EI'?

'i' before 'e', except after 'c', but only if the sound is 'ee'

If you are unsure whether a word is spelt 'ie' or 'ei', first ask yourself if it is pronounced with an 'ee' sound. If it is, you must put 'ie', except after a 'c' when the spelling is 'ei':

e.g. believe   chief   achieve   brief   field   siege   niece

and after 'c':

e.g. ceiling   receive   deceit   conceive   perceive

(The exceptions to this are: seize, weir, weird, protein, counterfeit, plebeian, caffeine and species. Also either and neither if you pronounce them 'ee'.)

A rhyme may help you remember the rule and the exceptions:

> 'i' before 'e', if you hear double 'ee's,
> Except after 'c' and in words spelt like seize.
> It's 'ei' in plebeian and 'ei' in protein
> And also in weird weirs and counterfeit caffeine.
> As for species – a word that is spelt to deceive –
> It's not 'ei' like ceiling, perceive and receive.

The reverse of the above rule is just as useful: **when the sound is not 'ee', the spelling is 'ei'.**

e.g. neighbour   height   weight   foreign   their   leisure
     heir

(The only exception to this is the word friend.)

'LONG' AND 'SHORT' VOWELS

The silent 'e' at the end of a word usually tells you that the previous vowel sound is pronounced 'long' (i.e. as in hope and tape, not 'short' as in hop and tap).

'long'	*'short'*
stare	star
pine	pin
slope	slop

• When you add suffixes like '-ing' to words ending in a silent 'e', the 'e' is usually dropped:

e.g. stare ....staring
     pine ....pining
     slope ....sloping

The silent 'e' is kept, however, when you add consonant-suffixes:

e.g. hope + ful ... hopeful   care + less ... careless

• When you add '-ing' or '-ed' to words ending in a single vowel followed by a single consonant, the last letter is doubled. (See chapter 9.)

e.g. star ....starring
     pin ....pinning
     slop ....slopping

(The exceptions are words ending in 'w' and 'x' like sawing and boxing.)

• In longer words a double consonant is usually a sign that the vowel before it is 'short':

e.g. 'short' as in supper (as opposed to 'long' as in super)

dinner	,,	,,	diner
furry	,,	,,	fury
holly	,,	,,	holy
comma	,,	,,	coma

(See chapter 9.`

COMMON ERRORS CAUSED BY PRONUNCIATION

Many common words are spelt wrongly because their pronunciation differs from their spelling or sometimes because they are mispronounced.

The part(s) of the word where the mistake usually occurs has been italicized. (In private you might try pronouncing these words as they are spelt, with an exaggerated emphasis on the part in italic type or on slurred or nearly silent letters.)

To help with persistently misspelt words, try to associate the word with another word in its 'family' or invent ways of remembering the spelling:

e.g. me*di*cine can be associated with me*di*cal, recog*n*ise with recog-nition, lux*u*ry with lux*u*rious, hypoc*ri*sy with hypoc*ri*te and democr*a*cy with democr*a*t.

e.g. I see A rat in sep*A*ra*te*.

(a) Stress the vowel.

- The following have an 'e':

  int*e*rested   list*e*ner   veg*e*table   gen*e*rally
  temp*e*ramental   temp*e*rature   lit*e*rature   math*e*matics
  arithm*e*tic   d*e*scribe   d*e*scription   d*e*spise   d*e*spair

- Concentrate on the 'i' in:

  def*i*nite   r*i*diculous   prim*i*tive   *i*nspired   *i*nvolve

(b) Pick out the 'lost' letters in:

di*a*mond   pic*t*ure   arc*t*ic   choc*o*late   Febru*a*ry
library   attem*p*ts   twel*f*th   fi*f*th

(c) A sense of the word's structure can help. See chapter 8.

e.g. govern ment – gover*n*ment   (Compare enviro*n*ment – environs.)

(d) Say these words very slowly, breaking them up into syllables:

con/tem/por/ary   lab/or/at/ory   sec/ret/ary   itin/er/ary
vet/er/in/ary   est/u/ary   Feb/ru/ary   part/ic/ul/arly
pec/ul/i/arly   simil/ar/ly   famil/i/ar/ly   stat/ist/i/cian
femin/in/ity   Wed/nes/day

(e) Exaggerate the italic letters in these normally slurred endings:

monast*e*ry   cemet*e*ry   station*e*ry (envelopes)
dysent*e*ry   imagin*a*ry   second*a*ry
murd*e*rous   boist*e*rous   thund*e*rous   sland*e*rous

43

(f) These are often mispronounced and therefore misspelt:

intellectual (no 'r' after the first 'e')
disintegrate (no 'r' after the first 'e')
mischievous (no 'i' after the 'v')
grievous (no 'i' after the 'v')
burglar (no 'u' after the 'g')
century (no 'a' after the 'u')
recognise (or -ize) ('cog' not 'ker' in the middle)
undoubtedly (not undoubtably)
et cetera (shortened as etc. – not 'ect'...)

(See chapter 11 for confused word endings.)

Test yourself (Cover the above when tackling this test.)

All of these are misspelt. Write out each word correctly:

reddiculous	definate	mannagable	boistrous
suprize	foregner	vetinerary	enviroment
charachter	deciept	littrature	picknicing
bileeve	perceeve	Wedensday	cemetry
panniked	exsitement	hypocracy	solemmly
chauvenism	beseege	contempory	admireing
Antartic	frend	sepperate	servisable
sheeld	hygeene	greivious	sheddule
monastry	primmative	swiming	vishus
knarled	neece	mischievious	seeze

(Answers in chapter 14.)

8

Roots, prefixes and suffixes

English spelling will seem much more logical if the formation and origin of words are understood. Breaking words up into their component parts and grouping them into 'families' according to their derivation are both obvious aids to spelling, as is an understanding of the main rules or practices governing word-formation.

ROOTS

Many English words contain roots or base-words (often derived from Latin, French or Greek words) to which are added prefixes and suffixes. For instance, the word 'interruption' contains the root 'rupt' (Latin for break or rip), a prefix 'inter' (meaning among or between) and a noun-ending or suffix '-ion'. The same root can be seen in: abruptly, rupture, erupted, disruptive, bankruptcy and corruption.

(Sometimes the root has more than one form – corresponding to the verb-forms of the original language – e.g. 'cid' and 'cas' are both roots from the Latin verb meaning fall or happen and can be found in words like incident, accident and occasion.

Knowledge of roots helps with the spelling of these words:

- the root 'sci' (know) in:
  conscious, unconsciousness, science, conscience, conscientiously

- the root 'fini' (end or limit) in:
  finish, finite, infinity, definite

- the root 'rid/ris' (laugh) in:
  ridicule, ridiculous, deride, derisive, derisory

45

- the root 'mit/miss' (send) in:

  admit, admission, permit, permission, permissive, commit, commission, commitment, intermission

- the root 'ceive/cip/cept' (take) in:

  except (meaning taken out), interception, perceive, perception, conceive, concept, deceive, deception, accept, receive, recipient

SOME OF THE MAIN PREFIXES, ROOTS AND SUFFIXES

(n. – noun, adj. – adjective, adv. – adverb, vb – verb. * – see *Prefixes which change*, below.)

Prefix	Root and Suffix	Word
a (from, away)	vert (turn) –	avert
ab (from, away)	horr (shudder) *ent* (adj.)	abhorrent
abs (from, away)	tain (keep) –	abstain
*ad (to, towards)	jac (lie) *ent* (adj.)	adjacent
ante (before)	ced (go) *ent* (adj.)	antecedent
anti (against)	dote (given) –	antidote
auto (self)	cracy (government) –	autocracy
bi (two)	sect (cut) *ion* (n.)	bisection
bis (twice)	cuit (cooked) –	biscuit
circum (around)	fer (carry) *ence* (n.)	circumference
*con (together, with)	tempor (time) *ary* (adj.)	contemporary
con (together, with)	sens (feel) *us* (n.)	consensus
contra (against)	dict (say) *ory* (adj.)	contradictory
contro (against)	vers (turn) *ial* (adj.)	controversial
de (down, away from)	tract (draw) *ion* (n.)	detraction
de (down, away from)	scribe (write) –	describe
de (down, away from)	scend (climb) –	descend
*dis (apart, not)	suade (persuade) –	dissuade
e (out of)	loqu (speak) *ent* (adj.)	eloquent
ex (out of)	cite (stir) *ment* (n.)	excitement
ex (out of)	hibit (have, hold) *ion* (n.)	exhibition
extra (outside)	vag (wander) *ant* (adj.)	extravagant

for (not)	bid (command) –	forbid
fore (before)	bode (promise) –	forebode
hyper (over, beyond)	tens (stretched) *ion* (n.)	hypertension
hypo (under)	derm (skin) *ic* (adj.)	hypodermic
*in (within, into)	cid (fall, happen) *ental* (adj.)	incidental
*in (not)	aud (hear) *ible* (adj.)	inaudible
inter (between, among)	ject (throw) *ion* (n.)	interjection
intro (within)	duce (lead) –	introduce
intro (within)	spect (look) *ively* (adv.)	introspectively
mis (not, wrongly)	spell (read out) –	misspell
*ob (in the way)	struct (build) –	obstruct
ob (in the way)	trude (push) –	obtrude
per (through)	secute (follow) –	persecute
peri (around)	scope (watch) –	periscope
peri (around)	meter (measure) –	perimeter
post (after)	pone (place) *ment* (n.)	postponement
pre (before)	cede (go) –	precede
pro (onwards)	pell (drive) *er* (n.)	propeller
pro (onwards)	fic (make, do) *ient* (adj.)	proficient
re (back, again)	cogn (learn) *ise/ize* (vb)	recognise (-ize)
re (back, again)	cur (run) –	recur
se (apart from)	para (set, make ready) *tion* (n.)	separation
*sub (under)	terra (earth) *nean* (adj.)	subterranean
super (over, above)	vise (see) –	supervise
super (over, above)	sede (sit) –	supersede
sur (over, upon)	prise (take) –	surprise
sym (together)	phon (sound) *ic* (adj.)	symphonic
syn (together)	chron (time) *ise/ize* (vb)	synchronise (-ize)
tele (far)	graph (writing) –	telegraph
trans (across)	port (carry) *able* (adj.)	transportable

Using a dictionary to check derivations, find other words containing the above roots, e.g. 'para' is also in preparation and apparatus.

(Sometimes words will contain several prefixes and suffixes, e.g. irrevocably contains ir (not) re (back) voc (call) ably (adv.).)

PREFIXES

1 Prefixes which change

Several prefixes, especially 'ad', 'con' and 'in', 'assimilate' or adapt to suit the sound of the first consonant of the root. This usually results in a double letter:

e.g. the prefix 'ad' (to, towards) and the root 'tract' (draw) form the word attract.

2 Common words with 'assimilated' prefixes include

ad (towards, to): abbreviate (brev – short), accelerate (celer – fast), accept (cept – take), accident (cid – fall), acclaim, accommodate (commod – fit with), accompany, accumulate (cumul – pile), accurate (cura – care), acknowledge, acquiesce (quiesc – rest), affect (fect – do), aggravate (grav – heavy), aggression (gress – go), alleviate (lev – light), allocate (loc – place), announce (nounce – message), apparatus (para – ready), approach (proach – near), approximate (prox – next to), arrange, arrears, arrest, ascertain, associate (soc – share), assume (sume – take).

con (with, together): collapse (lapse – fall), colloquial (loqu – speak), commit (mit – send), commotion (mot – move), correct (rect – right), correspond, corrupt

in (not or within): illegal, illegible, immature, immediate (med – middle), immigrate, immortal, innate (nate – born), irregular, irrelevant, irresistible

dis (apart): differ, diffuse

ob (in the way): occasion (cas – fall), occur (cur – run), oppose (pose – place)

sub (under): succumb (cumb – fall), suppress

3 Don't mix up these prefixes:

ante (before): e.g. ante-room, ante-natal
anti (against): e.g. antiseptic, anti-nuclear, antidote

for (not): e.g. forbid, forgo (go without), forsake
fore (in front, beforehand): forebode, forecast, forestall, forecourt

hyper (over, beyond): e.g. hypersensitive, hyperactive
hypo (under, beneath): hypodermic, hypocrite, hypocrisy

48

pre (before): e.g. predict, precede
pro (forwards): e.g. proceed

4 Prefixes added to the root 'ceed' and 'cede' (go)

A rhyme helps: With 'suc', 'ex' and 'pro'
　　　　　　　　 Double 'ee' must go.

e.g. succeed, exceed, proceed

Otherwise, the ending is '-ede'. e.g recede, precede, accede, inter-
cede, secede
N.B. But supersede has an 's'.

GENERAL RULES FOR ADDING PREFIXES AND CONSONANT-SUFFIXES

1 Prefixes and roots

Prefixes and roots are normally fitted together without adding or
subtracting any letters (except for *Prefixes which change* above):

e.g. dis + appear – disappear　　　mis + applied – misapplied
　　 dis + appoint – disappoint　　 mis + spell – misspell
　　 dis + approve – disapprove　　mis + shapen – misshapen
　　 dis + service – disservice　　 over + rule – overrule
　　 dis + satisfied – dissatisfied　inter + rupt – interrupt
　　 un + natural – unnatural　　　with + hold – withhold
　　 un + necessary – unnecessary

2 Consonant-suffixes

(N.B. See chapter 9 for the main changes involving *vowel*-suffixes
and words or roots which end in a vowel.)

When you add a *consonant*-suffix (e.g. '-ment', '-ness') to a root
which *ends* with a *consonant*, do *not* subtract or add any letters:

e.g. keen + ness – keenness　　 stubborn + ness – stubbornness
　　 mean + ness – meanness　　drunken + ness – drunkenness
　　 govern + ment – government

3 'l' as a general exception

In word-forming the double 'l' becomes single.

- The suffix '-ful' has only one 'l':
  e.g. careful   dreadful   hopeful   beautiful
- The prefix 'al' (from all) has only one 'l':
  e.g. almighty   altogether   already   although
- Double 'l' becomes single in:
  welcome   welfare   until   skilful   fulfil

(Exceptions: illness, stillness, wellbeing (or well-being), fullness (or fulness.)

Test yourself (Cover the above when tackling this test.)

All of these are misspelt. Write out each word correctly.

dissobey	protude	exibition	underated
overiding	skilfull	irisistible	conceeded
openess	hyperdermic	untill	alocate
acomodate	comision	consientously	oponnent
exeption	witheld	bankrupcy	seperation
proceded	frightfull	unoticed	concensus
subconcious	aquisition	infinatessimal	
misstrust	interupt	dissapointing	

(*Answers in chapter 14.*)

9

The main changes when adding suffixes

(This chapter is best taken in small doses!)

You've probably noticed that when you add a suffix such as '-er' or '-ing' to a word, a change often comes over the word itself. For instance, add '-er' to the word merry, and it becomes 'merrier'.

Here are some guidelines about the changes that have to be made to word-endings when suffixes are added:

CHANGING 'Y' TO 'I'

This happens when there is a consonant before the final 'y' (but not when you add '-ing'):

e.g. happy ....happier, happily, happiness
     merry ....merriest, merrily, merriment
     likely ....likelier, likelihood
     lonely ....loneliest, loneliness
     pity ....pitied, pitiful, pitiless (but pitying)
     marry ....married, marriage (but marrying)

But it doesn't usually happen when there is a vowel before the 'y':

e.g. monkey ....monkeys (not monkies)
     journey ....journeyed

(The exceptions to this rule are mostly one-syllabled words. Thus, when you add a suffix, shy becomes shyer, shyness, shyly, as do sly, spry and wry. Pay becomes paid and day becomes daily.)

CHANGING 'IE' TO 'Y'

A few common verbs change the 'ie' to 'y' before '-ing':

e.g. die ....dying
     tie ....tying
     lie ....lying

DOUBLING THE LAST CONSONANT

- This happens with short words which contain only one vowel before the final consonant:

e.g. hop ....hopped
     skip ....skipped
     run ....running
     swim ....swimming

(The exceptions are words ending in 'w', 'x' and 'y', like sawing, taxed and stayed.)

- In longer words which end with a single vowel followed by a consonant you only double the last letter if the stress is on the LAST syllable of the original word:

e.g. In the word 'prefer' the stress is on the last vowel. It therefore becomes 'preferred' and 'preferring'.

begin ....beginning
admit ....admitting
occur ....occurred, occurrence
regret ....regretted, regrettable

The last consonant is *not* doubled if the stress is elsewhere:

e.g. In the word 'offer' the stress is not at the end but on the vowel 'o'; it therefore becomes 'offered' and 'offering'.

happen .....happening
gallop ....galloped
benefit ......benefited

(Apart from words ending in 'l', the only exceptions to this part of the rule are worshipped, kidnapped and handicapped.)

- In words ending in 'l', double it regardless of where the stress is:

e.g. travel ....travelled, traveller
     quarrel .....quarrelling

```
cancel .......cancelled, cancellation
marvel ......marvelled, marvellous
```

(The only exception to this is (un)paralleled.)

The following jingle may help you to remember all aspects of this most useful of all spelling rules:

To double or not to double?

Oh, it's wining and dining and staring and sparing,
But winning and dinning and starring and sparring.
It's just one for the long 'un but two for the short 'un,
But for longer than one sound the rule needs some sortin':
    It's two in referring, preferring, deterring –
    The stress at the *end* is what keeps occurring;
While in offering, proffering, galloped and walloped
The last letter's single, 'cept in kidnapped and worshipped,
For these two, like handicapped, have double 'p'
(There's no logic in these, so learn 'em, all three).
    A second 'l' follows when adding to 'l',
    Be it quarrel, or travel, or cancel, or revel.
    Paralleled (or unparalleled)'s the only bar to this jingle –
    With two 'l's before it, the last 'l' stays single.

(N.B. The above rule does not apply to double-vowelled words like shouting and revealed.)

WORDS ENDING IN A SILENT 'E'

Whether you keep or drop the silent 'e' depends on the first letter of the suffix. If the suffix begins with a consonant, you must keep the e:

```
e.g.  care + ful ............careful
      hope + less ..........hopeless
      lone + ly ..............lonely
      sincere + ly .........sincerely
      advertise + ment .advertisement
```

(But this rule does not apply if the e is sounded as in simple, humble, probable and subtle, which form adverbs as simply, humbly, probably and subtly.)

(The main exceptions are: argument, ninth, truly, duly, greasy, and wholly.)

If the suffix begins with a vowel, the silent 'e' is usually dropped:

```
e.g.  care ..........caring
      come ........coming
```

argue ....arguing
forgive ......forgivable

(However, there are several exceptions to this. Words which end in '-ce' and '-ge' keep the 'e' so that the c and g remain soft, e.g. manageable, courageous, serviceable. The 'e' is kept, too, in singeing (burning), dyeing (colouring), swingeing (e.g. cuts) and routeing (directing). This is to avoid confusion with singing, dying, swinging and routing (defeating).

Verbs ending in -oe also keep the 'e', as in canoeing, hoeing, and the 'e' sometimes stays to stress the long vowel, as in mileage.)

DROPPING VOWELS WITHIN WORDS

Sometimes when we add a suffix a letter will drop out of the word itself. Thus, words ending in '-our' drop the 'u' when '-ous' is added:

e.g. humour ....humorous
vigour ....vigorous
glamour ....glamorous

In a similar way, generous becomes generosity; curious, curiosity; labour, laborious; but honourable does not drop the 'u':

Words ending in '-er' and '-or' also tend to drop the 'e' or 'o':

e.g. hunger ......hungry
enter ....entrance
hinder ......hindrance
disaster .....disastrous

(But there are several exceptions like boisterous, slanderous, murderess, adulteress.)

A similar change happens to words ending in '-nounce' and '-claim'. Thus, pronounce becomes pronunciation and exclaim, exclamation.

Test yourself (Cover the above when tackling this test.)

Add '-ing' to these:

tie	try	pummel	offer
argue	dye	incur	kidnap
manage	acknowledge	reclaim	benefit
toe	fulfil	murmur	prefer
carry	profit	differ	quarrel
suffer	fidget	defer	permit

Add '-ment' to these:
excite   achieve   argue   employ   merry

Add '-ness' to these:
lively   shy   weary   silly

Form adjectives ending in '-ous' from these:
vigour   courage   disaster   labour   outrage   humour
fury

(Answers in chapter 14.)

10
Adverb endings

THE NORMAL ADVERB ENDING IS '-LY' WHICH IS SIMPLY ADDED TO THE ADJECTIVE:

e.g. quick + ly – quickly   immediate + ly – immediately
extreme + ly – extremely   cool + ly – coolly
sincere + ly – sincerely   cruel + ly – cruelly
definite + ly – definitely   similar + ly – similarly

'-ful'/'-fully' (This follows the above rule.)

All adjectives formed with the suffix '-ful' have a single 'l'. When '-ly' is added a double 'l' occurs:

e.g. careful + ly – carefully   skilful + ly – skilfully
hopeful + ly – hopefully   successful + ly – successfully

'-al'/'-ally' (Again, this follows the above rule.)

Adjectives ending in '-al' add '-ly' to produce a double 'l':

e.g. final + ly – finally   incidental + ly – incidentally
actual + ly – actually   accidental + ly – accidentally
usual + ly – usually   occasional + ly – occasionally
real + ly – really   principal + ly – principally

EXCEPTIONS TO THE ABOVE RULE

'-ic'/'-ically'

Adjectives ending in '-ic' (e.g. basic, terrific) form adverbs in '-ically'. (Originally the adjective form was '-ical' as in the old word fantastical.)

e.g. basic – basically
      drastic – drastically
      terrific – terrifically
      tragic – tragically

pathetic – pathetically
frantic – frantically
scientific – scientifically
fantastic – fantastically

(The only exception is publicly.)

'y' to 'i' (See chapter 9.)

Adjectives ending in 'y' change the 'y' to 'i' before '-ly':

e.g. hungry – hungrily
      busy – busily

necessary – necessarily
extraordinary – extraordinarily

'-ble' to '-bly' and '-ple' to '-ply'

Adjectives ending in '-ble' and '-ple' (e.g. able and simple) form adverbs in '-bly' and '-ply' (e.g. ably and simply):

e.g. capable – capably
      legible – legibly
      valuable – valuably
      humble – humbly

probable – probably
terrible – terribly
ample – amply
supple – supply

Also subtle – subtly

truly, wholly and duly

true becomes truly, whole – wholly, due – duly

fully and dully

Three 'l's being impossible, full becomes fully and dull, dully.

Test yourself (Cover the above when tackling this test.)

Form adverbs ending in '-ly' from these:

plentiful	frantic	due	specific
public	probable	subtle	immediate
sincere	general	particular	skilful
actual	incidental	comic	unnecessary
complete	full	sympathetic	automatic

(*Answers in chapter 14.*)

11
Which ending?

'-ICAL', '-ICLE' AND '-ACLE'

(a) **'-ical'** is an *adjective* ending:
e.g. identical, technical, critical, physical
(b) **'-icle'** and **'-acle'** are *noun* endings, usually distinguishable by their pronunciation:
e.g. vehicle, icicle, article, particle
e.g. tentacle, spectacle, miracle, obstacle

'-ER', '-OR' AND '-AR'

These are noun endings meaning doer or agent. There is no rule, though '-or' is most common for people.

(a) **'-er'** tends to indicate an Old English word and to be used for the earliest and most basic occupations:
e.g. maker, baker, gardener
Note: character, propeller
(b) **'-or'** indicates a more modern activity or profession. ('-or' words are usually based on Latin or French words.)
e.g. doctor, author, solicitor, surveyor, professor, governor, conqueror, emperor, donor, vendor, sponsor, tractor, supervisor
(c) **'-ar'** There are only a few of these. Learn the common ones:
e.g. grammar (cp. grammatical), scholar (scholastic), calendar, burglar, cellar, caterpillar

Note: **'-ar'** can also be an adjective ending: e.g. similar, familiar, peculiar, particular.

'-ARY', '-ORY' AND '-ERY'

Again, there is no rule, though '-ary' and '-ory' tend to be the adjective endings, while '-ery' is a noun ending.

(a) '-ary':
- adjectives: imaginary, stationary (still), primary, secondary, voluntary
- nouns: library, dictionary, granary

(b) '-ory':
- adjectives: sensory, compulsory, supervisory
- nouns (indicating a place): dormitory, laboratory, observatory, lavatory, refectory

(c) '-ery':
- nouns: monastery, cemetery, stationery (envelopes, etc.)

'-TION', '-SION', '-SSION' AND '-CIAN'

The '-ion' ending means a state of being: the '-cian' means a person skilled at something (e.g. musician, mathematician, physician, statistician).

(a) '-tion' About six out of every ten '-ion' nouns have the '-*t*ion' ending which is usually pronounced 'shun'.

(If there is a verb from the word's family ending in 't' or 'te' or 'fy', the ending is usually '-*t*ion', e.g. educate – education, satisfy – satisfaction.)

(b) '-sion' This is usually pronounced 'zh'n' rather than 'shun'. Verbs ending in 'd' or 'de' form nouns in '-sion'
e.g. persuade – persuasion, collide – collision, pretend – pretension, comprehend – comprehension.

(c) '-ssion' The double 's' occurs when the root ends in a double 's'
e.g. possess – possession, profess – profession

Verbs with the Latin root 'mit' (send) form nouns with '-ssion'
e.g. permit – permission, admit – admission, commit – commission.
Similarly with verbs with the root 'cede/ceed'
e.g. concede – concession, proceed – procession.

'-OUS', '-EOUS' AND '-IOUS' (meaning full of or like)

(a) **'-ous'** occurs after a complete word ending in a consonant:
e.g. mountain – mountainous, danger – dangerous, peril – perilous

If the word ends in a silent 'e', this is dropped before '-ous':
e.g. ridicule – ridiculous but see (b) below.

Nouns ending in 'f' change to 'v' before adding '-ous'
e.g. grief – grievous, mischief – mischievous

(b) **'-eous'** The 'e' keeps the 'g' soft in
courageous, gorgeous, outrageous

The 'e' can be heard in plenteous and bounteous.

Learn these: simultaneous, miscellaneous, spontaneous

(c) **'-ious'** The 'i' keeps the 'c' soft in
spacious, gracious

and the 'g' soft in
religious, sacrilegious

Words ending in 'y' change to 'i':
e.g. fury – furious, envy – envious, vary – various, mystery – mysterious

(See chapter 9 for endings in '-*or*ous'.)

'-ENT', '-ANT'; '-ENCE', '-ANCE' AND '-ENSE'

Unless you have a knowledge of Latin verbs, there are, unfortunately, no guidelines, but '-ent' is more common than '-ant'.

(a) After a hard 'c' or 'g' the **'-ant'/'-ance'** endings will occur: after a soft 'c' or 'g' the **'-ent'/'-ence'** endings:

e.g. elegant, elegance, significant, significance
e.g. negligent, negligence, magnificent, magnificence

(b) **'-ent'** is the adjective ending in dependent and confident: '-ant' is the noun – a dependant, a pendant.

Some common words to learn:
relevant   perseverance   maintenance

sentence   existence   experience   excellent   competent
suspense   expense   recompense   immense

'-ABLE'/'-IBLE' (and '-ably'/'-ibly'; '-ability'/'-ibility')

Again, no rules, but **'-able'** is more common when the suffix is added to a complete word:
e.g. return – returnable, change – changeable, agree – agreeable

Where there is a verb ending in '-*ate*' (or a noun in '-*at*ion') in the word's family, the '-able' ending will also occur:
e.g. demonstrate, demonstration – demonstrable

'-ible' is common after 's' (e.g. feasible, visible, permissible) and if there is a noun ending in '-ion' (but not '-ation') in its family (e.g. audition – audible, combustion – combustible).
But indispensable.

'-ISE'/'-IZE'

The '-ise' ending is now more common and usually acceptable. Some like to keep the Greek-derived '-ize' for verbs with the sense of making or altering something (e.g. fertilize, legalize, recognize), but '-ise' is the 'safe' ending.

Test yourself (Cover the above when taking this test.)

Add '-er', '-or' or '-ar' to these:
emper—   govern—   gramm—   profess—   surviv—

Add '-ence' or '-ance' to these:
experi——   eleg——   persever——   exist——   sent——
excell——

Form adjectives ending in '-able' or '-ible' from these. Make any other necessary changes.
notice   comprehend   admit

Form adjectives ending in '-ous' from these:
religion   envy   plenty

Form nouns ending in '-ion' from these:
pretend   omit   apprehend

(*Answers in chapter 14.*)

12

Terms you need to know

VOWELS: the letters a, e, i, o, u, and y when it sounds like i (as in try and gypsy)

'short' and 'long' vowels: The vowel sounds in cap, met, sit, hop, cur and holly are called 'short'; those in cape, mete (measure), site, hope, cure and try are 'long'. (The signs ˘ for 'short' and ‾ for 'long' are used in some dictionaries.)

(A single vowel sound may consist of two letters, e.g. as in re*a*d, m*ai*n, c*ue*, pl*ou*gh; or a diphthong – now usually written ae and oe – as in an*ae*sthetic and man*oe*uvre.)

CONSONANTS: all letters except a, e, i, o, u. (y can be a consonant, e.g. in yes, beyond.)

'hard' and 'soft' consonants: Some consonants can be pronounced 'hard' or 'soft': e.g. The 'c' in cat is 'hard' (a 'k' sound) but it is 'soft' (like 's') in ceiling.

e.g. The 'g' is 'hard' in gun but 'soft' (like 'j') in gem.

(See chapter 7.)

SYLLABLE: a single sound containing one vowel sound

e.g. The word man has one syllable; separate has three syllables.

STRESS (or accent): in words of more than one syllable, one of the syllables or sounds is stressed

e.g. re*fe*r, *o*ffer, b*e*nefit, occ*u*r, pr*e*ference, pref*e*r

Many dictionaries use the mark ′ after the stressed syllable, or insert a space before it.

(See chapter 9.)

PREFIX: a group of letters (or a letter) added to the front of a word (or 'root') to alter its meaning

e.g. dis- un- anti- mis-

as in *dis*appear, *un*natural, *anti*-nuclear, *mis*spell

(See chapter 8.)

SUFFIX: an addition to the end of a word (or 'root') which alters its meaning or function

> e.g. -ness   -dom   -ment   -wright
>
> as in mean*ness*, wis*dom*, govern*ment*, play*wright*
>
> '-ly' is the usual adverb ending or suffix, e.g. sincere*ly*, immedi-ate*ly*
>
> **A vowel-suffix** is one which begins with a vowel, e.g. '-ing' as in beginn*ing* and '-ed' as in enjoy*ed*
>
> **A consonant-suffix** is a suffix which begins with a consonant, e.g. '-ment' as in argu*ment* and '-ness' as in stubborn*ness*

ROOT: the basic part of a word without any prefixes or suffixes

> e.g. 'voc'/'vok' (a Latin root meaning' voice or call) is found in these words: *voc*al, in*vok*e, e*voc*ation, irre*voc*ably
>
> (See chapter 8.)

SINGULAR: the form of a noun (or pronoun) which shows there is only one

> e.g. book, man, child, lady, bus, wife, valley

PLURAL: the form of a noun (or pronoun) which shows there is more than one

> e.g. books, men, children, ladies, buses, wives, valleys

HOMOPHONES: words with the same pronunciation but different meanings and, usually, different spellings

> e.g. pear, pair, pare; bored, board; principal, principle

PARTS OF SPEECH (i.e. the different jobs done by words):

(a) a NOUN names a person, thing or quality:
   e.g. boy, John, brick, beauty, decision

(b) a PRONOUN stands in place of a noun (to avoid repeating it):
   e.g. he, him, me, it, they, them, you, anyone, who, whom

(c) a VERB expresses an action (or state of being):
   e.g. he *ran*; he *is* ...; I *will go*
   (It has several tenses – e.g. past, present, future – which show when the action takes place.)

(d) an ADJECTIVE describes a noun (or pronoun). It can either stand in front of a noun or refer back to it:
   e.g. a *black* cat; *my own* work; the *quick brown* fox; the street is *long*.

(e) an ADVERB usually 'modifies' a verb, telling how, where, when or why an action is done. (It can also modify an adjective or another adverb.) Except for some very common adverbs, it usually ends in '-ly':

e.g. He ran *quickly*; *very* good; *extremely quickly*

(f) a CONJUNCTION joins, or shows the relationship between words, phrases or clauses:

e.g. fish *and* chips; poor *but* honest; for better *or* for worse; he played well, *although* he was injured.

(g) a PREPOSITION introduces a phrase and is followed by a noun or pronoun (which it 'governs'):

e.g. Put it *on* the table; *by* air; *up* the pole; *over* the hills; *between* you and me

(h) an INTERJECTION is an exclamatory word (or phrase). It can be taken out of the sentence without destroying the sense:

e.g. er; no; oh dear; ugh!

(A phrase is a group of words which acts as a noun, adjective or adverb.)

13

Dictations

(with the Speller family)

These five dictations are intended to be searching. It is best to prepare them first, though they may be attempted unprepared by more confident spellers. They are graded according to difficulty and are recommended as a final series of tests after the book has been studied.

Ask someone to dictate them to you about four words at a time, pausing for about ten seconds after each phrase, or record them in this way.

(a) Story-time with Minnie Speller

Oliver Oyster was lazily lying in the lap of luxury in his St Osyth oyster-bed, coolly cogitating among the calm currents of the Colne Estuary, while delightedly dining on a dinner of delicious delicacies. He was peacefully picnicking off his plentiful prey of plankton protein garnished with various invisible vegetables.

Opening his enormous mouth, which was wholly stomach as well, he mused aloud. 'It's quite quiet here. I can hear no one,' he murmured, and the echoes from his bivalves bubbled like balloons through the murky waters. 'I'm the direct descendant of the original emperor of oysters,' he simpered self-consciously in his solitary splendour. 'My ancestors have lain here for centuries. I am unique. In my very valuable view even two oysters would be one too many,' he arrogantly argued, gorging himself on more mammoth mouthfuls, 'and I really couldn't bear the life led by those common cockles. Not that the meanness of a mussel's existence is much to be preferred; and as for those plebeian, poisonous prawns scuttling about in that insufferable sand, why, theirs is a life-style whose squalor and degradation I can barely conceive. Here at least I'm troubled neither by foreign visitors nor noisy annoyances called friends and acquaintances. Undoubtedly, loneliness is sheer ecstasy.'

With a suddenness that allowed him no time even for an irritable exclamation of surprise, the ooze around him exploded in chaos and, before he knew what was happening, this serenely selfish shellfish was seized from his bed to appear next evening in gastronomic grandeur in a savoury seafood restaurant.

Oliver's terminal triumph, however, was unfortunately spoilt by the presence of six other oysters with whom he was compelled to be an extremely close neighbour in the stomach of a portly old gentleman from Colchester whose comment to his friend as he swallowed Oliver was:

> 'One's fun
> But seven
> Is truly heaven!'

(contains about 100 spelling problems)

(b) Miss Speller

Extremely disappointed by past failures in her attempts to obtain employment as a solicitor's secretary, Miss Speller became desperately conscious of her exceptionally embarrassing tendency to commit appalling spelling errors which, in spite of all her commercial experience, made her appear ridiculously illiterate.

Deciding, therefore, that her spelling was definitely a hindrance and likely to have a disastrous effect on her future career, she immediately passed a solemn resolution to pursue orthographical excellence.

This decision undoubtedly involved not only a change of attitude, but also modifications in the character of her formerly illegible handwriting. In fact, she found it necessary to buy a copy of *Spell it Right!* in order to acquire a thorough knowledge of the principles of spelling and to learn to recognise her own peculiar faults. With its assistance she was able to practise a series of rigorous exercises and to concentrate on her own persistent errors, even though this occasionally meant checking each separate word in particular sentences.

It is truly no exaggeration to say that she was agreeably surprised by the noticeable improvement that occurred.

(contains about 70 spelling problems)

(c) A report on R. U. A. Speller from his college tutor

Richard is to be complimented on applying himself so enthusiastically to his academic work: in fact, it is difficult to criticise his
achievements in this sphere. His undoubted intellectual ability and
commendably scholarly attitude have impressed several of my col-
leagues at the college.

From his work in English Language and Literature it is apparent
that he is both interested and knowledgeable. He can marshal a
forceful argument, as was shown in his winning speech in the annual
public-speaking competition. He is always prepared to express a
coherent opinion, while in his private studies he makes admirable use
of library resources. In spite of occasional weaknesses in punctuation
and grammar, his written work is generally excellent; and he has done
some particularly promising descriptive and humorous writing.

In mathematics he is proficient and conscientious and rarely loses
concentration. Although he took some time accustoming himself to
the statistics syllabus, which has superseded the arithmetic paper, he
is now beginning to work with confidence and accuracy. In science,
too, he shows keenness and adopts a disciplined approach, his work
having obviously benefited from careful preparation. His growing
assurance and familiarity with different scientific concepts are com-
plemented by a skilful and efficient use of apparatus.

On the games field he has acquitted himself honourably. Perseverance, endeavour and persistence in practising passing tech-
niques, allied to an innate sense of ball-play and immediate acceler-
ation once the ball has been passed to him, have allowed him to
develop into an impressive three-quarter; in fact, in his regular
appearances for the college team his exuberance, athleticism and
courageous defensive play in the face of some aggressive, indeed
vicious, tackling on the part of opposition teams, have proved invalu-
able.

Unfortunately, I have received adverse criticism of Richard's
unruly and irresponsible behaviour latterly. While I would not wish
to exaggerate what is probably a temporary reversion to boyish
mischievousness, it must be admitted that Richard has a low boredom
threshold, and after the latest interruption of lessons in the chemistry
laboratory – the eighth or ninth involving Richard, I am assured –
followed by excessively boisterous quarrelling with his peers and
wilful stubbornness when accosted by the chief caretaker, I have
regrettably decided to take the necessary disciplinary action.

I should appreciate your co-operation in this matter and hope that you can be present at an interview with the College Principal at 3 p.m. next Wednesday.

(contains about 140 spelling problems)

(d) From Mr Speller's correspondence

Dear Lord Capital,

We acknowledge the receipt of your highly esteemed enquiry concerning Monastery Tor and are pleased to supply the relevant information.

As described in our advertisement in the February issue of *The Professional Men's Magazine*, the property is ideally situated for luxury holiday accommodation in a pleasant environment. (We understand that planning permission has been granted for up to forty-eight semi-detached leisure villas.) The site enjoys an atmosphere of primitive grandeur and complete tranquillity (particularly since the re-routeing of heavy vehicles on to the new dual carriageway), as well as commanding exhilarating, panoramic views over moorland scenery and the picturesque West Sunnyshire valleys.

Alternatively, the property can be highly recommended as an exceptional opportunity to acquire valuable industrial or business premises on land easily accessible to the motorway. The property comprises the principal religious quarters and extensive dormitories with their ancillary services, together with the adjacent grounds (formerly, we believe, the monastery's allotments or, possibly, a cemetery). These, with the outbuildings which, like the monastery, are of considerable antiquity, though in a state of extreme dilapidation, are clearly scheduled for re-development. As far as we can ascertain, there is every likelihood that any factories built on the site would comply with the safety regulations, and the scheme will undoubtedly be eligible for the usual generous government grants.

We shall be most grateful for the opportunity to assist you in this matter, should you decide to proceed with the purchase. We shall be happy, too, to offer guidance on the various financial services and legal procedures involved, including surveys and mortgage facilities, and to recommend a reliable surveyor for an independent assessment.

Yours sincerely,
I. M. A. Speller

(While every effort has been made to ensure the accuracy of the foregoing particulars, this letter in no way constitutes a guarantee or agreement, and no legal liability can be accepted for errors or for any expenses incurred by the client during negotiations for the said property.)

(contains about 120 spelling problems)

(e) An imaginary newspaper article: interview with Ada Speller

'Elegant, glamorous forty-year-old career-woman whose marriage to successful estate-agent Ivor ...' Ada Speller would ridicule the male-chauvinist character of such descriptions, preferring to describe herself as a person of few pretensions, humorously sceptical of all hypocrisy and privilege.

A qualified doctor of medicine and practising psychiatrist, Ada Speller is also the eminent author of miscellaneous pamphlets on dyslexia.

While emphasising the need to recognise the condition, Dr Speller believes that the labelling of careless or lazy pupils as dyslexic appeals to some parents because it shields them from the reality of their children's deficiencies. A deterioration in spelling, she claims, is a contemporary phenomenon, comparatively rare until recently, one of the side-effects of an audio-visual age. She also perceives a correlation between dyslexia and the current preference for the 'Look-and-Say' method of teaching reading at the expense of the phonic approach. (The doctor's prescription, incidentally, for the simply idle speller is a daily dose of old-fashioned spelling practice.)

Dr Speller acknowledges the lack of a consensus over the definition of dyslexia but says that there is every possibility that the true dyslexic is suffering from some physiological or psychological disability. The sufferer is normally assessed first for defectiveness of vision since the condition sometimes entails an inability to focus on more than one letter simultaneously. Those acquainted with numerous case-histories stress the characteristic lack of co-ordination between eye and brain, paralleling the difficulties experienced by those who cannot distinguish left from right; in effect, this is borne out by the fact that compelling a left-handed child to write with his right hand can have a dyslexic effect.

Dissatisfied with the prejudice she sometimes meets, which occasionally amounts to an educational conspiracy against teachers of dyslexics, Dr Ada is earnestly campaigning for more collaboration with schools, and is vigorously canvassing support for more special-treatment centres. The handicapped child, she feels, should not be allowed to view himself as a failure and must not suffer harassment or be publicly humiliated, since this will merely aggravate his disability and lead to a sense of desperation. Ada Speller counsels a variety of methods sympathetically adapted to the needs of the individual, although her personal preference is for a systematic programme of teaching based on listening and speaking, a procedure which, she says, has definitely benefited many of her patients and brought them a sense of fulfilment from their progress.

(contains about 100 spelling problems)

14

Answers to tests

Chapter 3: Diagnose your spelling problems

1 (a) We don't know where we're going.
   (b) Are their friends there too?
   (c) There's no doubt that it is past her bedtime.
   (d) I wonder whose car that is and who's parked it like that.
   (e) Is this your doing? Look what you're doing!
   (f) It is far too hot to go to the cinema.
   (g) A piece of slate must have fallen off the roof.
   (h) Illness didn't seem to have any effect on her performance since she was still first past the winning post.
   (i) Let's consider the principal arguments in his speech.
   (j) They will all accept the invitation except John.
   (k) The fox was quite quiet, hoping to lose its pursuers by lying low under the bracken.
   (l) He lay there for hours before anyone noticed him.
   (m) Do you need spelling practice?

2 ladies   thieves   oxen   dinghies
   valleys   businesses   spoonfuls   buses
   wives   chimneys   factories   potatoes
   allies   volleys   phenomena   passers-by
   heroes   ponies   vetoes   cargoes
   criteria   roofs   shelves   lorries
   crises   children   similes
   chiefs   sheep   echoes

3 mischievous medicine   vegetable   recognise
   interesting burglar   government   (or -ize)
   generally   intellectual ridiculous   February
   surprise   century   separate   undoubtedly
   secretary   laboratory   literature   involved
   peculiarly   library   terrifically twelfth

| hypocrisy | mathematics | in front | description |
| definitely | contemporary | (2 words) | primitive |

4 achieve conceit weird retrieve
belief receive height hygiene
deceit sieve friendly relief
besiege neighbour protein ceiling
seize sovereign freight briefly
perceive counterfeit heirloom grievance
handkerchief fiendish niece
weigh species piece

5 definite interruption antidote acknowledge
drunkenness dissatisfied excitement immediate
disappoint disappear proceed opponent
unnatural overrule succeed commotion
stubbornness careful accelerate irregularly
withheld environment forecourt acquire
welfare dissimilar illegible
skilful fulfil committed

6 exceptionally fantastically extraordinarily peculiarly
drastically publicly incidentally occasionally
beautifully truly coolly immediately
accidentally carefully sincerely invaluably
hungrily fully faithfully pathetically
humbly probably tragically successfully
really unnecessarily subtly
similarly frantically wholly

7 (a) supplied carried dried pitied surveyed
    enjoyed copied conveyed
   (b) marrying surveying supplying tying dyeing
    denying delaying trying lying singeing
   (c) loneliness liveliness prettiness tidiness
   (d) shyest prettiest loneliest likeliest slyest
    gayest busiest hungriest

8 (a) caring forgiving canoeing queuing pining
    mimicking sloping arguing manoeuvring
    achieving dying picnicking liking pursuing
    coming noticing admiring managing re-routeing

72

(b) achievement   argument   encouragement
(c) believable   noticeable   changeable   forgivable
(d) duly   lonely   immensely   truly

9 (a) courageous   glamorous   advantageous   laborious
     slanderous   mysterious   gracious   furious
     humorous   outrageous   vigorous   religious
     marvellous   disastrous   luxurious
   (b) serviceable   practicable   knowledgeable
     agreeable   permissible   valuable   changeable
     divisible   collapsible   honourable
   (c) extravagant   significant   elegant   negligent
     magnificent

10 swimming   occurring   beginning   quarrelling
   scaring   regretting   dining   concealing
   profiting   referring   preferring   paralleling
   fitting   emitting   admitting   galloping
   deferring   developing   transferring   kidnapping
   benefiting   propelling   riveting   pocketing
   committing   cancelling   omitting
   offering   worshipping   murmuring

Chapter 4: Test yourself

1 Whose is it? It's mine. Let's see. There you are then. But you're
 cheating. There's nothing there. Where did you hide it? I don't
 know. It must have slipped through my fingers.

2 There is no doubt that their singing is not what they're famous for.

3 He had already gone past me before he passed me the ball.

4 This tooth is so loose that I shall probably lose it.

5 If he lets us then let's do it.

6 There were too many for all of us to have a game.

7 They agreed to accept all the entries except mine.

8 We all need to practise our spelling.

9 Yesterday he was lying in the bed where he had lain for the last
 two weeks, but today the nurses have laid him on a sunbed
 outside.

10 His principal concern was for the legal principle involved in the
 case.

Chapter 5: Test yourself

1 Our local stationer's seems to sell a lot of Christmas gifts and children's games, whereas yours doesn't.
In spite of all the English team's efforts to recover their lost form, no one (or no-one) managed to score, although the team was playing in front of a home crowd.
The Women's Institute has, in fact, already held its annual meeting.

2 bases   tomatoes   journeys   taxes   piccolos   volleys
aches   follies   laboratories   roofs   storeys   send-offs

the ships' cargoes   the thieves' knives
the witches' prophecies   the children's ponies

Chapter 7: Test yourself

ridiculous	definite	manageable	boisterous
surprise	foreigner	veterinary	environment
character	deceit	literature	picnicking
believe	perceive	Wednesday	cemetery
panicked	excitement	hypocrisy	solemnly
chauvinism	besiege	contemporary	admiring
Antarctic	friend	separate	serviceable
shield	hygiene	grievous	schedule
monastery	primitive	swimming	vicious
gnarled	niece	mischievous	seize

Chapter 8: Test yourself

disobey	protrude	exhibition	underrated
overriding	skilful	irresistible	conceded
openness	hypodermic	until	allocate
accommodate	commission	conscientiously	opponent
exception	withheld	bankruptcy	separation
proceeded	frightful	unnoticed	consensus
subconscious	acquisition	infinitesimal	
mistrust	interrupt	disappointing	

Chapter 9: Test yourself

tying	trying	pummelling	offering
arguing	dyeing	incurring	kidnapping
managing	acknowledging	reclaiming	benefiting

toeing　　　fulfilling　　　murmuring　　　preferring
carrying　　profiting　　　differing　　　quarrelling
suffering　　fidgeting　　　deferring　　　permitting

excitement　achievement　argument　employment
merriment

liveliness　shyness　weariness　silliness

vigorous　courageous　disastrous　laborious　outrageous
humorous　furious

Chapter 10: Test yourself

plentifully　　frantically　　duly　　　　specifically
publicly　　　probably　　　subtly　　　immediately
sincerely　　　generally　　　particularly　skilfully
actually　　　incidentally　　comically　　unnecessarily
completely　　fully　　　　　sympathetically　automatically

Chapter 11: Test yourself

emperor　governor　grammar　professor　survivor

experience　elegance　perseverance　existence　sentence
excellence

noticeable　comprehensible　admissible

religious　envious　plenteous

pretension　omission　apprehension